The Miracle of Change

....

*Transforming the
Impossible into
the Possible*

DOUG ANDERSON

**TURNING
STONE
PRESS**

First published in 2013 by Turning Stone Press, an
imprint of Red Wheel/Weiser, LLC
With offices at:
665 Third Street, Suite 400
San Francisco, CA 94107
www.redwheelweiser.com

ISBN (paperback): 978-1-61852-061-6

Cover design by Jim Warner
Cover image: Getty Images

Printed in the United States of America

10 9 8 7 6 5 4 3 2 1

*The goal posts have moved in the game of life.
All the players are winning and the disappointed
spectators are sitting unhappily on the sidelines.*

Contents

Part Four

Dedication

*To those of you who know there
has to be a better way to treat each
other—a way of peace, abundance,
and prosperity. And especially to you
business and organizational leaders
who are feeling called to pioneer this
new way: it is time; you are the
one you have been waiting for.*

Acknowledgments

My guides, angels, family, friends, mentors, coaches, and trainers, Chuck and Lency Spezzano of Psychology of Vision, my editor Christine Yates, and all those who have shown me a better way, I love you. Thank you to Jesus, Buddha, Mohammed, and all the other prophets and teachers who came with instructions on how to live a life of love. My inspiration came essentially from their teachings; I think we are finally listening with an open heart.

God bless Joanne Roberts. She has flown to Vancouver many times to teach the Steps to Leadership to our small group! Without her, who knows where I would be today? From the bottom of my heart, I thank her.

Many friends, mentors, and trainers within the POV organization have had a major impact on my transformation to date and to you I am grateful. Thank you.

Why I Wrote This Book

My intention is to empower all people, leaders, businesses, and organizations to create change that vibrates with the positive shift that is happening on our planet.

This shift, I believe, is to a more peaceful existence, a happier planet, and a world that we'll wake up to every day saying, "Thank God I am alive!"

My passion is world peace through inner peace, and The Miracle of Change philosophy is part of my intended contribution to world peace.

The Miracle of Change calls on people to be models and mentors, to be willing to let go of what no longer serves them in this new paradigm, and to share their journey with those who trust them.

Here's what you can experience by putting the ideas in this book into action:

> Freedom to choose your life every step of the way;
>
> Release from old traps and beliefs you have used to avoid success;
>
> Joy, happiness, and success you never thought possible, in all areas of your life;

Recognition that your pain comes from
resisting change;

Guidelines and skills that will teach you
how to create the life you truly want and
desire.

May you open to all that is being offered you each and
every moment of each and every day.

Preface

This is a story about my own journey as a change agent for the paradigm shift we are going through here on planet Earth.

It's December 2011, and I am sitting here in my home office in Sechelt, British Columbia, feeling warmth and gratitude for finding my way to the hope, beauty, and choice that is now resonating within me.

I was born with a silver, or, as some of my friends would say, a golden spoon in my mouth, and yet somehow I never really believed the golden life in my heart.

Materially speaking, my world has been full. At times I have seemed to lose everything, yet the money and material possessions have always come back. I've learned what it was like to have and to not have. Even at the times of not having, a thread of "golden spoon" energy has run through my life.

I am a pioneer, a warrior, a leader, and a risk-taker. I've had both challenging and rewarding experiences, but in the end my life seems to come full circle every time. No matter where I go, there I am.

My passion is business and leadership coaching, sharing empowering solutions with other people who are feeling the call to be a leader for positive change in their lives, businesses, and communities.

This book is about empowering you to create lasting change in your life; change that will bring happiness to you and those in your world.

My wish for you is that you find the courage to choose your passion, to model that passion, and to mentor others in your world to do the same.

Game Guidelines

Sharing: Share yourself and see everyone playing their best game.

Caring: Care about others and help them when you can.

Love: Love yourself and those around you. No matter what, find a way to forgive yourself and those who irritate or appear to harm you in some way. Understand we are all doing the best we can with what we have.

Game Tools

Willingness: Willingness to get in the game and be open to changing the way you think.

Commitment: Commitment to the truth of who you are, in your natural state.

Awareness: Awareness that it is only when everyone wins that we align with our happiness and allow others this opportunity as well.

Acceptance: Accept what is, and also that there has to be a better way to live our lives.

Track Your Results as a Player or Spectator Using Your Daily Life Relationships, Events and Situations

- What Happened?
- Did I choose to be a: Player ( ) (or) Spectator ( )?
- How did I feel?
- Am I feeling?
- What was (is) the Result?

Part One

There is a whole new world out there, just waiting to be discovered. This unheralded new world is unfolding. It's up to me to be curious enough to look for it, willing enough to find it, and courageous enough to live in it.

❧ 1 ❧

There's a New Game in Town

A FEW YEARS AGO, it became clear to me that there is a feeling generally, among many people, that we need to improve the way we relate to each other. I noticed that the people who embraced this desire were experiencing greater levels of ease, happiness, freedom, and success.

In February of 2008, when hiking in one of my favorite parks, Cliff Gilker, here on the Sunshine Coast, I had a vision of two soccer teams playing. Everyone was happy and supporting each other. Both teams were enjoying playing the game and no one was keeping score. All the players were winning and having a great time. Their aim was to play the best game possible, and it seemed that each team was extending this intention to the other. What mattered was having fun and enjoying a great game.

The fans, on the other hand, were getting frustrated. They were feeling left out, unhappy, and restless. As I watched, it became clear that the only losers were the people in the stands who depended on their team of choice to win so they could feel happy, excited, and somehow fulfilled.

As the game went on, I saw people leaving the stands and joining the players on the field. Some of the onlookers decided that if there was no importance to the score and anyone could play, then they would rather be in the game.

I also witnessed the people who stayed on the sidelines becoming more irritated and angry; they were the only ones losing. On the field it appeared everyone was winning and happy.

I gradually understood that the vision was a metaphor for what is happening in our world and on our planet. People are starting to realize that winning has nothing to do with the score. Winning comes from playing the game with love and respect.

The Miracle of Change Benefits

As in the metaphor of a soccer game, in life, people who leave the stands and head onto the field to play in an atmosphere of love become relaxed, and start to understand how to enjoy life.

The players' lives do not necessarily come without challenges, but their new perception of how to handle the challenges is the game changer. By changing the way they play the game, people experience a more meaningful existence. They let their victim or victimizer stories go, and they experience much more freedom and happiness.

The guidelines of the game are sharing, caring, and love, and the game tools are willingness, commitment, awareness, and acceptance. Living with those guidelines and tools changes the emotions, thoughts, and expectations that most people learn from birth, and they start to experience love from within, as Marianne Williamson describes in her book *A Return to Love*.

For me, the soccer game vision was an inspiration to change my own perceptions and to get in touch with my emotions, thoughts, and desires to rid myself of mistaken beliefs about how the world had treated me. It's been quite a ride. I found myself on a journey through my subconscious and unconscious minds, and learned that I had been dissociated from both for most of my life. What I found, to my amazement, was that therein lay all my treasures and demons, and the path to freedom from the chains that bound me in my life.

Groundwork

It's possible that I would have dismissed the vision of an unusual soccer game as just a weird daydream if it hadn't been for the groundwork laid over the previous twenty-five years.

I have always had an easy time with work and the jobs I chose, and early on found myself climbing quickly into leadership positions. My first job was a paper route, which turned into two routes and the paper shack in my parents' garage. No matter if it was cooking, commercial hardware, or real estate, I experienced the same pattern of success.

I was nearing thirty when curiosity led me to inspirational inner-journey books and a teacher here and there. Despite a growing awareness of a different way of thinking, I continued to mistreat myself with excessive cigarettes and liquor and lack of exercise.

As I ventured further and further within my mind, the challenges grew more intense and the breakthroughs more grace filled. My life was improving, but there was still some unhappiness. I knew my heart had shut down, and I wanted to open it.

A Life-Changing Decision

My father died in June of 1983. Four years later, in the spring of 1987, my mom moved back to Nova Scotia from Vancouver to help her aging aunt live out her last few years in her home. As it turned out, Mom was there for two years before Aunt Maureen passed on.

Mom and I had always had a cold and hard relationship, not knowing how to be ourselves with each other. We were, for the most part, nice, dead people around each other, willing to do the right things for the wrong reasons and really just trying to stay out of each other's way.

Don't get me wrong, we had laughs and good times, and both my parents provided me with a good home and all the opportunity that I wanted. We travelled together, ate dinner as a family, and had a few pets (a cat or two and my favorite little pound hound Nicky, our one and only dog).

But I was an angry child and never let my parents off the hook. I was rebellious, fought with them constantly, and punished them, and me, with overeating. I played small and insecure and manipulated them and others by playing the victim or victimizer. In my teens, eating turned into smoking and drinking.

When my mother moved to Nova Scotia in 1987, something told me it was time to change my relationship with her. Something inside me needed to express the love I had for my mom.

I had to start somewhere. So, one day when she called and we'd had our usual chat about Auntie and the weather and family, at the end of the conversation, instead of saying goodbye and hanging up the phone, I said really quickly, "I love you Mom," and then hung up. It was awkward, almost embarrassing, and I thought, *Wow, was that ever a tough thing to do.*

As our calls continued over the next two years, each time we talked it got easier and easier to tell my mom I loved her at the end of the call. Eventually, after a year or so, one day my mom replied, "Me too," and hung up.

We were on our way. By the time Mom moved back to Vancouver, we could both say "I love you" on the phone. I cannot remember when we were able to say it to each other in person. It must have been in the '90s at some point.

With that one gesture, my heart opened a crack and my journey inward began. I was well on my way to exploring the road between my mind and my heart.

A Dramatic Lesson

I will never forget October 1, 1998. It was the day I quit smoking. I came home from work and was having dinner when I heard loud screaming coming from next door. Julie and Norm had been my friends and neighbors for two years and I'd never heard them fight. So I thought, *Mmm, good for them to let off a little steam*, and carried on eating.

Then the phone rang and it was Julie asking me to come over. Now, faced with a possible marital dispute between my friends, I thought, *Dear God, give me strength*.

When I got there, Norm, head down on the dining room table, was speechless, and Julie was pacing frantically around the living room yelling profanities at the top of her lungs. It was clear that something much more serious than a minor family dispute was going on. Julie stopped long enough between profanities to tell me that their thirty-year-old son had just died in a truck accident up north.

I sat there and loved them both; there was nothing to say. I thought that if losing a son created that much pain for a mom and dad, I couldn't do that to my mom. I quit smoking.

The Journey Begins

That year I quit smoking, my drinking subsided to a casual drink now and then, and I started to get more interested in my physical health. Two years later, I started going to a woman named Ileana, a Healing Touch practitioner recommended by my sister. Healing Touch is energy work similar to Reiki.

Over the next eight years, I let go of so much anger and other buried emotions lying on the treatment table as Ileana moved her hands above my body, clearing emotional and energy blockages from my chakras. For the most part, I had no idea what was leaving my body, but I knew for sure that I was shifting to a happier, safer me.

In March 2007, I left my twenty-two-year real estate career and started training to become a life coach specializing in leadership training and business coaching. Later that year, I was referred, again by my sister, to a woman who offered a Psychology of Vision (POV) "Steps to Leadership" course in Vancouver. The experience was the next step in opening my heart. That sometimes painful process of letting go of old thoughts and beliefs and remembering the truth of who I am couldn't have happened without the love and help of many trainers, coaches, mentors, and friends.

Psychology of Vision is a path of the heart that has helped tens of thousands of people around the world improve their lives. The model teaches accountability as a key tool. Taking responsibility for our own lives means we have the choice to change what is no longer working for us. As we remove the blocks that have been holding us back in our lives, our awareness grows, and we move more easily toward achieving our goals. Our relationships become happy and our lives successful.

Psychology of Vision's Steps to Leadership training program offers students the tools needed to transform their lives and, in doing so, the lives of the people around them.

The past four years of my journey with POV have been the most challenging and rewarding of my life. I am deeply grateful to Chuck and Lency Spezzano from Hawaii and to my main coach, Joanne Roberts, from Prince Rupert, British Columbia.

It's my feeling that as every day goes by, and as the level of consciousness rises on our planet, our transformation process is getting easier and more graceful.

Game Changer

I love the term game changer! Every time I get a new trick or easier way to shift from fear to love I call it a game changer, and it sure is. It's about forgiving myself when I fall off the proverbial horse and getting back into this ancient game.

As in my vision, I encourage you to follow your heart and inner guidance and get out onto the field of your life and play.

Have you found yourself noticing that something is changing in your life? Have you felt like the world around you is shifting, and that perhaps these changes are speeding up? Do you feel a difference that is tough to describe? Well you are on the right track.

❦ 2 ❧

It's Time to Play

M Y FEELING IS THAT WE, the human race on planet Earth, are kind, caring, and loving by nature, and at some level that's how we would like to live. It's time to unite and recreate our lives to reflect that desire at home, work, and play. It's time for each of us to become agents of change. It's time to play a game that everybody wins. It's time to use The Miracle of Change game guidelines, tools, and questions!

Anyone who follows the game guidelines and uses these tools can change their life, and ultimately the world, for the better.

The Miracle of Change Game Guidelines and Tools

Game Guidelines

> Sharing: Share yourself and see everyone playing their best game.

> Caring: Care about others and help them when you can.

> Love: Love yourself and those around you. No matter what, find a way to

forgive yourself and those who irritate or appear to harm you in some way. Understand we are all doing the best we can with what we have.

Game Tools

Willingness: Willingness to get in the game and be open to changing the way you think.

Commitment: Commitment to the truth of who you are, in your natural state.

Awareness: Awareness that it is only when everyone wins that we align with our happiness and allow others this opportunity as well.

Acceptance: Accept what is, and also that there has to be a better way to live our lives.

Come Play with Us

There are easy and not-so-easy ways to get involved in this new game. Choosing to be a spectator has little or no reward. Sitting on the sidelines waiting for someone else to make you happy doesn't work. In The Miracle of Change, only the players, playing by the new game guidelines and tools, reap the benefits.

So really it's your choice: continue playing by the old rules of competition, winner takes all, or go for hope and come play with us!

The need for this game is being fueled by a universal shift in consciousness. To play, you need only be aware, willing, and committed to doing the work. Everyone who chooses to be a player has the chance to make life rewarding and satisfying beyond belief. The Miracle of Change also inspires and motivates players to share their experiences with others. Friends and family who notice a positive difference in you want to know what has changed, and why you seem so much happier.

As I said, this game has tremendous benefits that filter through everyone playing and their personal, business, and community lives. Once you start playing, the game slowly becomes a way of being rather than doing. At that point, The Miracle of Change gives you access to unlimited inner resources to use and share with others.

Choosing to Be a Player or a Spectator

Players are those who choose to use the game guidelines and tools set out in this book. A player who finds themself in a competitive situation, for example, can choose the guideline Sharing to share their inner self and see everyone playing their best game. Players can also use the game tool Awareness to remember that it is only when everyone wins that we align with our happiness and allow others this opportunity as well. The game tools can be used at home, at work, at leisure, and when participating in sports. Try to think of your life as a game and the shift here will be much easier for you.

When you feel hurt, misunderstood, or ignored, you can use the game tool Acceptance. Accept what is, and also that there has to be a better way to live our lives. And you can choose the guideline Love—love yourself and those around you. No matter what, find a way to forgive yourself and those who irritate or appear to harm you in some way. Understand we are all doing the best we can with what we have.

When a spectator, on the other hand, finds them-self in a competitive or hurtful situation, that person just keeps doing what they have always done, and loses out on the opportunity to experience positive change. As you choose to become a player, look at your situation and pick the game guideline or tool that best fits, and try it out. Experience what happens as you try on the various game guidelines and tools in the different situations in your life. The same goes for when you choose to be a spectator—experience what happens. This is called research. You get the results firsthand!

Tracking your progress in The Miracle of Change is paramount to your success. Keeping a record of your daily situations and answering the following questions will help clarify your experience, and your progress will empower you to stay in the game. You'll soon see the value of using the game guidelines and tools.

Tracking Your Results as a Player or Spectator Using Your Daily Life Relationships, Events, and Situations

The Miracle of Change: For Life, Your Life		
What Happened?	What Happened?	What Happened?
Did I choose to be a: Player ( ) (or) Spectator ( )?	Did I choose to be a: Player ( ) (or) Spectator ( )?	Did I choose to be a: Player ( ) (or) Spectator ( )?
How did I feel? Am I feeling?	How did I feel? Am I feeling?	How did I feel? Am I feeling?
What was (is) the Result?	What was (is) the Result?	What was (is) the Result?

I have created this simple form to help you record your progress and to keep you on track. It is available on my website as a PDF download free of charge: *www.21stcenturydynamics.com.*

When you choose to be a spectator, experience how it feels and look at the results.

When you choose to be a player, experience how it feels and look at the results.

A quick review will help you to track your successes. Keeping a record of the answers to the above questions will empower you to keep recommitting to the game of your life, and will allow you to see the rewards of a different way of thinking and being.

There is a new paradigm unfolding. The Miracle of Change will assist you in aligning with this new paradigm to create more ease, flow, happiness, health, and abundance in all areas of your life.

Never Give Up

I have heard this important axiom throughout my life. It finally stuck in the late '80s when I heard it from my fellow realtor Lionel Lorence, and the impact has been with me ever since. I am sure it is one of the building blocks to success in many areas of my life.

Be Willing

Another bit of wisdom that comes to mind is about being willing. Be willing to be wrong; to find a new way; to let go of old pain; to try something new. In my experience, every time I choose to take a risk, there is a safety net and the way through gets easier, more rewarding, and happier each time.

Change Is You

When you choose to be in the players' box, you are well on your way to being a winner, playing with winners, and assisting and empowering other people to win. Players have unlimited access to abundant resources!

When we choose to go back to the spectator section, our challenges increase, stress levels go up, and happiness goes down because we're using the old fear-based reasoning to deal with whatever is wrong. The negative approach often leads to poor health and depression. People either stay stuck and hang on for a rough ride, or they're motivated to get back in the game. In no time, the switch through forgiveness to a positive outlook, supported by positive changes, improves the ease and flow of everyday life and levels of health and happiness.

So most of us get back in the game as soon as we become aware that life has taken a downturn because we are sitting yet again in the stands, spectating.

What Now?

Where to from here? It's all choice, and while you are choosing please feel free to switch back and forth between sitting in the grandstands as a spectator and getting into the game of your life as a player. This is an effective way to feel and witness the difference between the two.

Keep in mind that I am sharing with you a vision of a new ancient game that came to me in 2008. The game as I see it is new, but the knowledge behind it has been with humanity since the beginning. This game is a metaphor for life. Keep an open mind and be willing; when you experience the results of using the game guidelines and the tools you will become aware that it is possible to live in a way that creates freedom to be yourself and live in the now.

It's up to you how and when you go about integrating the game tools and guidelines into your life, but if you give The Miracle of Change an honest try you won't be disappointed. Everyone knows that the world needs someone to make a change for the better.

Part Two

The fear of change is an illusion, false evidence appearing real. The first time we experienced change, it was a negative experience, an experience of separation. No wonder we fear change so much!

⮞ 3 ⮜

If It's Going to Be,
It's Up to Me

AT THE GYM WHERE I WORK OUT, the sign on the wall in front of the treadmill I like to use reads, "Please stay off the plastic rails on the sides of the track as they are costly to replace. Thank you for your cooperation." I can't help looking at the sign every time I'm there, which is often. One particular morning, a new message popped into my mind. I saw instead, "Your cooperation is appreciating."

Then another thought came in: "And adding value to your life and those around you." As I stayed with the feeling, it became clear that the message I was receiving was all about cooperation versus competition. My next thought was, if cooperation is appreciating and adding value to my life and those around me, then competition must be depreciating and devaluing my life and the lives of those around me.

So, in the game of life, when I cooperate with others my stock goes up, and when I compete my stock goes down. Mmm, I thought, *this is brilliant, another game changer!*

The Miracle of Change in Action

A few years ago a friend of mine, Ali, and I started playing racquetball. Ali was new at the game, so most of our matches were an easy win for me. Ali was several years younger and in great physical condition, so as we played more he started to win the games. In keeping with the game guidelines and tools in this book, I sent him thoughts of support and winning. I saw him playing his best game ever and genuinely cheered him on in my mind.

Gradually, several new moves came in, I had more energy, and I started to win more games again. I told Ali my secret weapon, and he always just smiled. I have no idea if he ever tried using the same technique of supporting me or not, but I kept winning, and at the same time I was seeing him playing his best, sending thoughts of support, and cheering him on in my mind.

Then, one day, he won two out of three and I congratulated him. He was so happy. I asked when the next game would be and he said, "Let me savor this for a while." Ali has not called back for another game. When he does, I will again see him winning and will support him to have his best game ever.

For those of you in professional sports, business, leadership or any other activity where competition has been the main focus, heads up. There is a better way. Are you appreciating your stock and the stock of those around you by cooperating? Or depreciating your stock and the stock of others around you by competing? It's your choice. It's a new paradigm.

Remember the game guidelines and tools. Apply them, and you are naturally cooperating at home, work, and play.

The Power of Choice

Choice. I talk a lot about choice and choosing in this book for a very good reason. Without the power of choice, how could we change what we are not happy about?

Choice is where most of us have been running on automatic. We may choose one item over another in the store, or what we plan on doing with our next project or the next event to entertain ourselves. But when it comes to what is not working for us in our lives, we run on automatic. We think that the direction our life takes is determined by something outside of us, that our lives are shaped by something other than the power of our own choice.

When we go on automatic, our decisions come from our subconscious and unconscious minds. Since we are, for the most part, dissociated from those parts of our mind, we feel that life just happens to us, and that we have no choice or control in the matter.

Well guess what? You are the boss of you. This is another life-changing idea. The good news is if we have the power to choose, then we have the power within us to change. We can change whatever is not working in our lives, businesses, organizations, families and communities.

Choosing to be a player gives you easy access to undo the traps in your subconscious and unconscious mind. Then, through forgiveness, a willingness to be wrong, and giving of yourself, you can take charge and take responsibility for your life.

Life transforms into a much happier, more prosperous, and more fun and enjoyable existence when we start cooperating, loving others, and recognizing that, just as we are, they are doing the best they can with what they have. As players, we recognize that we have just as many blind spots as the next guy or gal, and that we are all in this game together.

Spectators sit on the sidelines or in the grandstands and let life happen to them. Players use the guidelines and tools. This process helps create a habit of choosing how our lives unfold. We make room for love by releasing past pain through sharing ourselves and our gifts with others, and by forgiving ourselves and others when we feel hurt. Ninety-eight percent of our hurt or pain comes from our past, from our unconscious and subconscious minds. Old hurts, family dynamics, and ancestral patterns can be healed when we dare to face them, accept them, and forgive.

We are here to find a better way of being—this is evolution. It is my belief that one of our soul promises before we came to Earth was to save our family. To love them back to the truth of who they are and stop blaming them for being wrong. This takes courage, and the rewards are immense, beyond anything that we can imagine. Most of us forget this promise and fall into victim or victimizer traps, feeling that our parents do not love us. While, all along, we are the ones who promised to bring the love and heal our family.

So we got it all mixed up. No big deal. Forgive yourself and get on with your original promise of loving your family back to happiness.

We heal ourselves and our families by recognizing our past hurt and pain, then forgiving the source and understanding that if they could have been different, they would have.

We as humans tend to repeat patterns in our ancestral chains. So, if we feel victimized at some point, we later become the victimizer. The abuse pattern is clear in the history of our planet. Countries, people, communities, and organizations have all acted out a terrible pattern of insanity at one time, and many of us feel we have no way out. But we do. We have the power to choose forgiveness, to share our gifts, and to live in love.

Life, and our world as we know it, is shifting rapidly from a fear-based paradigm to a love-based paradigm, and the greater the number of people willing to do the work to open their hearts and minds to cultivate kindness and goodness, the easier the change will be.

You, the change agents, are needed now more than ever before in the history of our planet. You are the ones you have been waiting for. Make the choice today to use forgiveness and be a player, a change agent for peace and prosperity.

The Power of Forgiveness

My friend Chuck Spezzano, cofounder of Psychology of Vision, has shared the following story a few times over the last several years in workshops that I have attended. Yet, it has taken literally years for the message to really hit home for me, integrating into my heart and mind with full understanding. Today, I feel it in my heart.

I hope Chuck's story touches you as well:

> When I was a boy, I watched hundreds of cowboy shows, but only one stayed with me over the years. It was about a sheriff and a gunslinger. Every year the gunslinger came back and threatened to terrorize the town. Each year the sheriff would meet him on Main Street, shoot the gun out of his hands, arrest him, and send him off to jail.

Then one year the sheriff hung up his guns, vowing never to use them again. Once again, the gunslinger came back, threatening violence to the town. The retired sheriff met him on Main Street because no one else had the courage to face him.

When the gunslinger saw that the sheriff had no gun, he called the sheriff a coward and told him to come back when he had his gun. The sheriff refused, saying he'd hung up his guns forever.

All the time they were talking, the sheriff was slowly walking toward the gunslinger.

The gunslinger said, "Well if you're not going to get your gun, I'll just have to kill you," and taking his gun out, he shot the sheriff in the arm.

The sheriff was pushed back by the shot, but after a moment continued toward the gunslinger, who then shot him in the other arm. Again, jolted back, the sheriff once more continued toward the gunslinger, who shot him in the leg. The sheriff went down, knocked to the ground, looked up and, without hesitation, began crawling toward the gunslinger. The gunslinger shot him in the other leg, felling him completely, and the sheriff lay flat. But still, after a long moment, the sheriff looked up and began pulling himself forward with his forearms.

At that moment, the gunslinger dropped his gun, rushed to the sheriff, and threw his arms around him, completely disarmed.

A shopkeeper in the background turned and said to a bystander, "That's the bravest thing I ever saw."

When I was a boy that was the bravest thing I ever saw.

There is great change going on in our lives and on our planet, using The Miracle of Change game guidelines and tools may be the ticket for an easier ride. Surf the wave of change, be a player, and enjoy the ride!

⌒ 4 ⌒

Play Like You Have
Nothing to Lose

FOR MOST OF MY LIFE, I have been quite a conservative guy. I've been bold and forthright at times,
but most of the time beneath the brass is shyness and a
feeling that I'm not good enough. It was an eye-opener
for me when the POV workshops and training gave me
access to the insecurity buried in my subconscious. It was
POV that helped me to start healing those parts of my
mind. Through that training, forgiveness, and studying
"A Course in Miracles," I have learned that if something
has to change in my life, I'm the only one who can make
the change happen. A Course in Miracles teaches that
the way to universal love and peace is to let go of guilt
and forgive others. For more information, check out
www.acim.org.

By being able to access the parts of my mind that hold
on to past wounds, I have an opportunity to acknowledge
and accept them, perhaps forgive myself and whomever
I've blamed, and let the anger go. Exposing fear through
acceptance, as well as feeling my anger and emotions,
removes the charge and takes me another step or two

toward my center, a place of balance and peace. I am more willing to take chances and to be me—another step toward loving myself and just enjoying being myself! The more I am willing to let go and trust, the happier I become.

Remember, it's all choice. When I feel blocked or held back, at some level in my mind I have chosen it that way. This may be a tough pill to swallow, but in time you will learn that by using the guidelines and tools in this book, you can choose to be happy and actually feel it happen.

My friend Iain and I ski at Whistler Blackcomb near Vancouver in the winters, and we have fun challenging each other to take the next step and let go a little more. Iain is usually gently nudging me to take a chance, and every time I do I experience more freedom, less fear, and a greater sense of happiness.

Iain loves to take me on steep T-bar lifts and windy chairlifts to the very top of mountains, and sometimes beyond the tops of the lifts, where we hike up steep terrain. From there, he just drops off the edge and disappears. My heart goes into my throat and I feel the fear. I stand at the top of a run so steep that I cannot even see past the edge, and I have no idea what I will be skiing into. I wait as the fear turns to courage, and I slide over.

Once committed, I have a blast. The fear subsides and oh boy, what a feeling. Some times are more challenging than others, yet every time it gets easier and easier to let go, drop off the edge, and trust it will all work out. I am grateful for my friendship with Iain for many reasons, and his stretching me beyond where I thought I could go is one of them.

The Miracle of Change

Stories Can Hold You Back

I can still, at times, get caught up in the stories in my life. When that happens, the old, negative thought patterns have the effect of blocking my ability to choose to see things differently. They also block my willingness to be wrong about my perception of the stories. I am choosing to stay stuck.

Some of the stories I have let run through my head in the past (and still do when I forget to be a player) go like this: somebody did something bad to me on purpose to get back at me or to get under my skin.

Other stories are more complex, and have deep plots of conspiracy, manipulation, and betrayal. Some seem innocent, yet when I am honest and look closely, there is still a bad guy, or I am still defending my position in some way.

These are all just stories, and they keep me trapped.

When I am not willing to be wrong about my stories, and when I refuse to look at them another way, I can stay stuck in the same negative pattern for a long, long time. This is what I refer to as insanity. That's right, insanity! When I am stuck like a gerbil on a wheel of victim or victimizer thoughts and emotions, I am actually acting out an insane part of my mind.

Using the game guidelines and tools in this book, feeling my emotions, and choosing forgiveness and love changes my perception; the story collapses into a totally new understanding of the person and situation.

This is what I call a "miracle." I change my perception and my stories change; my life naturally aligns with what is good in my world, and I am my happy self again!

Let's have a look at an easier way for me to go through my day. The second I am willing to be wrong, everything changes. My mind opens up to all possibilities. I'm open to other interpretations of what happened, so I am able to take in *all* the information, feel my feelings, and be discerning.

Now, this does not mean I go into sacrifice and let others run all over me. It means I get beyond my narcissistic side, stand back, and assess situations with all my senses before deciding my next move. When I choose to be a player, I gradually open my heart and dissolve the insanity. I also become a safer, happier person to be around. I drop the need to hang onto my anger and fear, and default to a more balanced and peaceful state, which is my human heritage.

The fun begins here—when I choose to be a player I come alive, recognizing I truly have nothing to lose and everything to gain.

≈ 5 ≈

Question Everything

ONE THING I HAVE FOUND in my life is that when I follow a person or a program without questioning, at some point I get uncomfortable and fall into judgment. I have followed many masters and programs, and when I forget to question the teacher or idea, I get confused and give away my power of choice. From there, I become a follower and not a leader. I become susceptible to dogma, blind spots, and others' untrue agendas.

The leaders, in most cases, are innocent and do not even know they are taking me down a path that may be true for them and not true for me, but I've learned that it's important to remember to trust my intuition.

Why am I rambling on about this?

First, because when I question a person or idea it gives me an opportunity to test the integrity of what is being presented according to what I know to be true for me. From here, I can assess and discern if it is in my best interest to continue, or if it is more in keeping with my own values to make another choice.

Second, when I decide to give it a go after due consideration, the resulting experience has great power and can lead to a healing breakthrough. By questioning everything, I stay mentally and emotionally balanced, become more solid in my understanding, and build trust in my own instincts and heart to guide me.

Question with an Open Heart

When I use the term "to question" something or someone, I am talking about using the energy of curiosity. I question with an open mind and an attitude of willingness, then depending on how I feel, I choose to continue or not. When I ask questions and share my experience, I open the door to receiving the clarification needed to make a good decision without blaming or making anyone else wrong.

The times in my life when I have followed a program or person blindly, my lessons have been to get back into my own power and stand up for myself. The experience of giving my power away was so uncomfortable that I was compelled to find my real feelings and to follow what I knew to be true for me. In the end, although all of that is difficult, the result is real learning about who you are and how you want to live.

For example, a few years after I'd decided to focus on personal development, I chose to join an organization that empowers people to create change in their lives. On the very first day of our two-day weekend course, I got it! I got that the weekend was all about teaching me that I choose the things in my life, both positive and negative.

I stood up, went to the microphone, and said in disbelief, "All this time, all my life, everything that has happened to me has been my choice?"

I was blown away. It was such a powerful awareness for me. That understanding was for sure another game changer.

As the day and weekend unfolded, I got more confused. I felt like the program was pushing me to conform to a set pattern, and I totally forgot the epiphany of that first morning.

Before the last segment Sunday night I ran into one of the staff in the hallway and they asked me how I was doing. I said, "You cannot let me outta here in this state, I am so messed up and confused."

He said, "Perfect, you are in a great place for this last segment."

Somehow his words calmed me, but I was far from a place of feeling empowered. There was one more segment to finish off the weekend, and the presenter said we could invite the person who had recommended the program to us to join us for this final part.

There were two or three hundred people in the room. My friend was with me and it was time to pick someone from the group to come onstage as an example. Yes, you guessed it, I was picked. So, up front I went and parked myself in the swivel chair onstage next to the trainer.

He said, "Are you willing to play with me here?" I said yes.

He said, "Now, you may be the last person in the whole room to get this . . ." I accepted that this could be my fate.

He started the exercise by asking me, "If I offered you a chocolate or vanilla ice cream cone, which flavor would you choose?" I answered chocolate. Then he asked, "Why did you choose chocolate?" I said, "Because I like chocolate." He went on and asked more similar questions and I answered in the same way. The crowd laughed more and more as they got it, and yet I was blind to the point of the exercise. This went on for ten or fifteen minutes.

Another angle, more questions, more laughter, and I was still not getting it. Then, I finally broke out laughing as I understood the point. I choose chocolate because I choose chocolate and that is that! Experiences are positive or negative because I choose to experience them as positive or negative experiences, and it's that simple.

The whole point of the exercise is to make it clear that we do choose everything in our lives because we choose it—period. Once we understand and accept that, we start to recognize where we have choices and can consciously decide to think or do what is best for ourselves and others. Now I felt great, just like I had on the first morning of the program.

I signed up for the next course. It was another weekend event with a smaller group, perhaps ninety to a hundred people. This time I was sold on the program and stopped questioning, just as I had after the initial discovery in the first weekend. I dove into becoming a follower and swallowed the teachings whole.

Gradually, I became increasingly uncomfortable, and as the third program over the next few months unfolded, I realized I was following without questioning and had given away my power. As that awareness grew, I got so uncomfortable that the only relief was to share with them that I no longer wanted to continue with their organization.

My lessons again were to stay in my power, get into my center, and question everything with a sense of curiosity.

In reflection, I think that the whole point of taking their training was to build trust in myself. Their recruiting and marketing was heavy duty, and anyone who did not pull up their power could easily get caught up in it.

I believe all things happen for me to learn a lesson and return to love. If you open your mind and question everything and everyone with an attitude of curiosity, you will have an opportunity to become more heart centered and discerning.

The Miracle of Change Is No Exception

When you're using the game guidelines, tools, and questions in this book, stay true to yourself. Question everything, be aware, and feel what it is like to be both a player and a spectator. Make a conscious choice of which you will be in each situation. You might decide to be a spectator at times. Remember, everything you do is a choice, no one else is choosing anything for you.

When you choose to be a player, you are sure to feel the difference. Pull up your power, be curious, be willing to give it a go, and notice what happens in yourself, in the people around you, and in your life.

One thing that I have experienced over the last few years is that every time I have changed my mind through forgiveness, love, and sharing myself, the people around me change for the better too. The most dramatic and miraculous change is in the people closest to me. When I change my mind, my world changes right along with it; this is what makes playing The Miracle of Change so worthwhile and rewarding.

Above all, be you. You are the one you have been waiting for.

～ 6 ～

What If?

ONE OF THE MOST POWERFUL tools I use in
my life, and when I am coaching and training, is the
question "What If?"

What if I'm willing to be wrong about someone or
something?

What if I am willing to try it, just this once, and see
what happens?

What if there is another way?

What if there is a better way?

A powerful and life-changing statement that I have
learned and use, when I remember to, is, "Above all else,
I am willing to see this differently."

In my experience, when we start to turn our thinking around and let go of what has kept us from being at
ease within ourselves, some resistance to that change can
come up and we can dig in our heels.

An internal fight often arises between the ego that
believes competition is necessary to survive, and the
heart that knows love is the best way. The ego can give us
the very uncomfortable feeling that we are letting someone off the hook who really did us wrong at some point in
time and ought to be punished.

Yes, it may appear that they did something to hurt us, but, what if?

What if I was seeing the situation with limited sight, with, say, only 3–5 percent of available insight, and I made assumptions from that vantage point, or that disadvantage point?

I am not asking you to believe me, I am asking you, "What if?" That's all.

What if you have the capacity within you to open up to 100 percent of your insight, awareness, and understanding? Would you be interested?

One hundred percent insight is the power of "What if?" If nothing else guides you along the path of positive change, let it be this one powerful question: "What if?"

Changing Your Mind Can Save Your Life

My dad died in 1983 when I was twenty-three years old. He was a healthy guy most of his life, and at the age of fifty, while in the shower one day, he experienced a brain hemorrhage. Six years later, he died just before his fifty-seventh birthday.

This would change our family's lives forever. Dad was down and on his deathbed and we were shocked.

Early on in his health crisis, the doctors found that his kidney function was very low. They told us he had Polycystic Kidney Disease and would require dialysis and possible transplant should he survive the brain hemorrhage. He survived and became a kidney dialysis patient.

Then the doctor said there was a possibility that one or more of us three kids may have the same disease as Dad. When the testing was finished, we were told it was me; I had Polycystic Kidney Disease.

Our family doctor at the time was not too concerned, as my kidneys were functioning very well. He said that by the time my kidneys started to fail, technology would have advanced, and there would most likely be a cure or an easy remedy for me.

As the years went by, I forgot about, and certainly did not worry about, my kidneys being at a disadvantage. It was not until the early 2000s that I decided I could use alternative or holistic healing methods to heal my kidneys. I received Healing Touch, acupuncture, massage, and chiropractic therapy. I tried Qigong, Tai Chi, and meditation.

My determination to heal my kidneys through alternative and holistic methods was strong, and I was unwilling to consider dialysis or transplant. My mind was set: I could heal this, period.

Despite feeling that alternative healing methods were enough, I joined the pre-transplant clinic at St. Paul's Hospital in Vancouver in 2003 to monitor the results of those methods.

In the summer of 2006, I was just about to leave my house and head up the coast on my motorcycle when the phone rang. It was my older sister. She and I were a match for transplant, and she had a message, an offer, and some insights for me to consider.

At this point I was down to around 15–17 percent kidney function in total from both of my kidneys. The great thing about kidneys is that they operate very well down to about this range or even less.

My sister was calling to encourage me to consider transplant. I was still very rigid and not willing to look at the situation differently; I was still determined I could beat this thing and heal myself.

She told me, "You were born in this part of the world where there is state-of-the-art technology and medical help at your fingertips at no or very little cost. Combining alternative, holistic, and eastern healing models with the western medical model may be something to consider. And, I am offering you my kidney."

I started to cry. I was willing to consider. What if?

What if what my sister is sharing is the truth for me?

What if all this stubborn, well-intentioned determination to heal myself is not the answer?

What if there is another way?

I broke down, I surrendered, and I accepted this precious gift of a healthy kidney from my sister.

On February 27, 2006, my mom's and my nephew's birthday, my sister and I walked into St. Paul's Hospital in Vancouver at 8:30 a.m., and by 6:00 p.m. I had three kidneys and my sister had one. Thank God I surrendered and allowed the question "What if?" to be considered. I was down to 10 percent kidney function just before the surgery; I was never on dialysis.

The transplant was a success and both of us were up and out of the hospital within five days. The healing was well underway for both of us, and I left eight months later on a two-and-a-half month Mexican camping trip. The clinic was not impressed, but I had something to celebrate!

With my new kidney, my new health, and my new freedom, my life was at a major turning point, I could feel it, and all because I was willing to consider, "What if?"

Whenever I catch myself being defensive, digging in my heels, or determined to be right, I am willing to reconsider, "What if?"

What if I am wrong?

What if there is a better way?

What if I'm not seeing the whole picture?

I encourage you to try asking yourself "What if?" in your daily life. Track the results and see for yourself: there's an easier, happier way waiting for you, as you're willing.

❧ 7 ❧

The Power of Simplicity—Your Wild Card

A LL OF MY LIFE I HAVE known that keeping it
simple is best for me. This philosophy has worked
well for me generally, but especially in my career, business, and group activities.

Did I always keep things simple? No. But when I did,
and when I do, life sure gets easier!

I tend to see issues in a simple way, using both intel-
lect and intuition, which allows me to consider possibilities and offer a useful solution to whatever is not working
so well.

One of the ways I keep things simple is to ask the
following question: Can a ten-year-old child understand
what I am saying? Or, in the case of a team, what we are
saying? This exercise has lead to great success in my team-
building and business ventures.

Two of the most successful ventures I have been
involved with were selling residential real estate and
cofounding a local charity in my hometown of North
Vancouver, British Columbia.

My real estate career was spread over twenty-two years: eleven years in North Vancouver and eleven years on the Sunshine Coast.

In keeping with my motto of staying simple, I would ask these questions: What is really going on here? What do we need to do next? What is the easiest and best way to handle this? And, most importantly, can a ten-year-old child understand what we're proposing?

A Lesson in Simplicity

The year of 1991 was another wake-up call for me. I had gone overboard in my spending habits and had gone into debt to buy cars, houses, and trips. In my mind, I was living the all-American or Canadian dream. I was young, successful and had a great career in the real estate world. One of my goals was to become a millionaire by the time I hit thirty years old. Too bad I forgot to set the intention for a million in cash and assets, not debt!

I had created almost a million dollars of debt, and, as a result, my whole life had to be simplified. At the same time, the real estate market was slowing down, interest rates were above 11 percent, and I had a very expensive lifestyle to maintain. I was reduced to two basic functions: survive and trust. First went some real estate holdings, then a car, then my savings.

What saved me was the ability to pay my bills. I got by with one of my many credit cards and unexpected refunds or checks of some sort that showed up in the mail. I was still running a team at work, and somehow we all made it through. I learned about trust, miracles, and the power of debt. I was getting an upgrade in keeping things simpler, and also some insight into a part of me that was crying out for help. Crying out for love.

In the middle of all this turmoil, I met a woman who was teaching A Course in Miracles, and I have no idea to this day if she ever read the text or did the lessons. Regardless, she helped people to open their hearts and experience a spiritual awakening.

The one thing I learned from her was to tithe. *Tithe*, I wondered, *what's that?* It had never occurred to me to give to strangers in need, from my heart! Unconditional giving was a new concept for me.

This woman taught me to feel into my heart for where I am called to give, and then to do it without expectation of any return. I knew instinctively it was the right thing to do, and went looking for a place to tithe.

Soon after that commitment, at the worst point of my financial crisis, as I was taking from one credit card or line of credit to pay another, I read about a guy who was starting a charity in North Vancouver to help others in need of food, clothing, shelter, and work. My heart said that this could be the place to start.

The fellow I had read about agreed to meet me at my office and the next thing I knew, I was part of the start-up team. I joined the Board of Directors and committed to giving this group 10 percent of my income, my income that was barely keeping things afloat. Yikes!

I made the leap and trusted that the woman who was teaching me to give from my heart was leading me down a path of more ease, happiness, and flow.

The charity work lit me up. It was an amazing feeling to give happily of my time and money and to create from love. Our charity's motto was "Giving a Hand Up . . . Not Out."

We started the organization in the back of a clothing warehouse in North Vancouver in 1991. I became chairman of the board, and five years later the organization had gross revenues of well over half a million dollars a year, and we were giving a hand up to hundreds of people in need.

Again, one of the gifts I brought to this organization was simplicity: Can a ten-year-old understand this? I encouraged our group with questions such as, what is our next step? How can we better serve the people we are here to help? How can we empower them to give back in their greatest time of need? That philosophy helped guide and set the direction for this success story.

When I forget to keep things simple, it gets tougher to get through my day and I tend to get caught up in the story of the problem or issue and become a victim or victimizer rather than a solutions guy.

The Simplicity of Forgiveness

As the years have passed, I have come to understand and appreciate another simple way of staying on track. One of the simplest ways of creating more ease and flow in any endeavor is to forgive. It also saves enormous amounts of time, money, pain, and hassle.

Forgiveness makes everything better for me and for those around me, usually in an instant. When I am angry, in fear, or feel that someone has done something hurtful to me intentionally, forgiveness shifts me into peace and understanding.

As we learned in The Miracle of Change game guidelines and tools, life is all about deciding whether to be a player or a spectator. Which one makes me happier?

Forgiveness is simple, but I'm not saying it's easy. In fact, forgiving another person who has hurt us can be the toughest thing we ever do! How can such a life-changing, life-enhancing, loving, caring thing like forgiveness be so hard at times? Forgiveness can be hard when we believe in our mind and body that someone deserves to be held accountable for whatever happened, and we refuse to see them as innocent.

During my senior year at high school, I walked about half an hour or so to school. No big deal. Yet, many days my mom drove by me on my way home, and when I waved at her to stop she didn't see me and just kept on driving. I took it personally that she could just drive by and not see me. I became angry and irritated and judged my mom. How could she not see me? What a so-and-so.

It was easy to forget all the good things my mom did for me every day. Instead, I focused on a few key injustices and that would plug me into anger over and over again. When I look back over my early life, situations and stories changed, yet the same dynamics were at play. I loved my mom and then I hated her, I loved my mom and then I judged her. I wanted to love her unconditionally, yet something was standing in the way, something in my mind and emotions that I just did not understand.

I judged my mom for ignoring me and for being cold and emotionally unavailable. In my younger years, I also judged her for being the tough parent in our family, always saying no.

When I was about ten years old, I decided that my mom and dad did not love me anymore because they quit hugging me before I went to bed. I decided that Dad had no time for me, and I took the gloves off. I started smoking at the age of twelve, and was a very angry kid. I blamed my dad for being too conservative, not spending time with me when I was younger, and being too aggressive. I was getting my revenge.

When I was thirteen, Dad started to make great efforts to bond with me again, but I would have nothing to do with him. I rebelled against all efforts he made to hang out with me and repair our relationship.

Dad passed away when I was twenty-three, and the rebellion went on right to his passing, playing itself out in many ways over the years. Dad would extend himself to me and I would reject his efforts. We would get along okay for a while, and then something would trigger my anger again and we would drift far apart. He would get frustrated with me and I would reject him. It was a repeating pattern.

One day, when I was eighteen or nineteen years old, my sister let me know that Dad was concerned I was on drugs. He felt my behavior around him and my resistance to wanting to hang out with him was driven by drugs. In truth, I was holding on to a past story and was punishing him for it.

The pattern carried on into his business, where I joined him in the last two years of his life. We'd get along, then fight. There were misunderstandings and rejections, over and over again.

The Tools of Forgiveness

In the intervening years through my studies and experiences with Psychology of Vision and A Course in Miracles, I have come to learn a lot about how the human mind works. Over the past five years, this learning has opened me up to a whole new way of looking at my life, and an understanding that what actually happened may not be the same as my perception of what happened.

I have learned that most of my pain and hurt came from judgments, misunderstandings, and attacks on my parents. I forgot that if they could have done it differently, they would have. I forgot how much they loved me. I did not see that they could only love me to the best of their capacity at the time, and I gave them no rope for being human. I had no idea that they were being run by their subconscious and unconscious minds just as I was, and that they had no idea what the heck was going on either.

It is my understanding that when we come into this world, we have good intentions to bring light and love to our family and the planet. I also understand that most of us forget this most important part of who we are, and become conditioned by the world around us at a very early age. I had forgotten that it was my promise at a soul level to bring love and my unique gifts into my family when I was born, and to continue to fulfill that promise throughout my life here on our planet.

They forgot, and I forgot. The whole thing had been one big misunderstanding, repeating itself from generation to generation. In other words, when I forget that love is who I am, the only way back to remembering is forgiveness. It is that simple!

It is my belief that each generation has done its best and chipped away at making this world a better place. Some previous generations have been aware of the need to check perceptions and to forgive others. Unfortunately, not enough of our ancestors in any generation had the collective understanding needed to create a global shift to peace. Now all of us together have the opportunity to create a new paradigm of peace on planet Earth.

Forgiveness Heals

So why is it so hard at times to forgive? Because buried deep in our subconscious and unconscious minds are beliefs, thoughts, and experiences that we have hidden from ourselves. When something similar happens and triggers our emotions, if not the memory, we bump up against the fear and anger of those experiences without understanding what is happening, and we react and over-react automatically. Those dark places in our minds are waiting to be filled with love, waiting to be understood, accepted, forgiven, and set free.

Until we unearth, forgive, and let go of our buried beliefs and thoughts from our past experiences, these beliefs and thoughts continue to run our lives from the inside out. They are projected onto the world around us, and we have no clue what's happening. Life seems to be happening to us. No one has ever told us, no one has ever given us this life-changing information—or have they? And we just did not understand or listen?

When it's hard or impossible to forgive someone or something, you can be sure that you're stuck in fear, anger, and revenge from past hurt and pain, possibly from as far back as conception or even past lives. Use this new understanding to change your thinking. Then you can take action and forgive. When we choose not to forgive, we choose to stay trapped in pain. It's that simple.

Remember, we are in the middle of a paradigm shift, and the game is changing daily to a more loving, caring, and sharing environment as more and more people decide to choose forgiveness and love. Without forgiveness, there is no hope when we fall out of love.

By playing The Miracle of Change game and experiencing yourself as a player sometimes, and a spectator at other times, you will have the opportunity to get into a new awareness mode. You will discover that you can actually witness and monitor your thoughts. This is powerful, life-changing information: what you think can set you free should you choose to take the risk and be a player.

Reflections

Some say that our world is a house of mirrors, meaning that what is going on around us is a reflection of what is going on inside of us. The behavior of people in the world outside of you is a clue to what's going on in your own subconscious and unconscious mind. It is your choice what you do with this information. Knowing that your environment is talking to you in a sort of code can make your life much easier once you have the key to the code.

Your friend who is acting angry and judgmental just may be showing you clues about yourself. Rather than judging them, trying to settle them down, or getting involved in the drama, say to yourself, "Can I feel this anger inside me right now? Can I recognize where I have been judging others?"

Going into quiet gratitude at this point helps you get in touch with your own anger and judgments. Staying calm through feeling your own emotions, regardless of how they are acting, will help you and your friend. With courage and willingness, you can explain to your friend how they are helping you to get in touch with your own emotions. Go into quiet gratitude again, knowing your friend is acting out your anger so that you can heal yourself.

The explanation almost always has an unexpected calming effect on the person who is upset, so if they ask what you just did, share about The Miracle of Change and your experiences. Make it about you and no one else.

Do you question how that all works, exactly? Well, when you think about it, how the heck else are you ever going to get in touch with your subconscious and unconscious mind to free your emotional blocks if the world around you doesn't act it out for you?

Once you see yourself in the mirror of those around you, you can choose to start playing differently. You can lay down your need to judge, blame, and punish others for acting out these parts of your mind by choosing to forgive yourself for those feelings, and being grateful to the person who showed you that part of yourself.

Once you can wrap your head around this new information and start using it to create new levels of ease and flow, you are well on your way into life in the new paradigm. By using the game guidelines and tools in this book, you can heal your past and make available more of your gifts to share with others.

You may need to take a few deep breaths here in order to digest this new awareness. Let it sink into your being and trust the feeling. Know that with willingness and determination, you can create a more abundant and peaceful life.

Really, I am sharing with you an ancient truth about life. This is not new information; it has been around for eons, yet not embraced by the majority of people. Choose forgiveness in the present moment to heal and let go of past pain.

Ninety-eight percent of what causes us to feel miserable is wrapped up in the past. How we get along with people in present situations reflects how we judged parents, siblings, and others in similar situations in the past.

Remember when I shared the dynamics and judgments I experienced with my mom? I will continue to project those judgments onto other people until I can heal that past pain in the now!

Forgiving in the present moment shifts a situation from negative to positive, helps to heal the past, and gives me a whole new outlook and understanding of what really is going on.

My willingness to use this knowledge has transformed many areas in my life. I've been able let go of past emotional blocks, and the result is a whole new way of being for me—healthier, happier, freer, and more abundant than ever. The process is taking me away from feeling like a victim, and is removing my need to victimize or judge everyone in my life now the way I used to judge my parents, siblings, and others.

Tracking your results as a player or spectator using your daily life relationships, events, and situations will help you experience for yourself a difference between your relationships now and your past relationships. For me, the changes have led to more ease and grace with my current relationships.

As I've said, past hurts and misunderstandings are stored in the subconscious mind. The easiest way to heal and release buried hurts is to forgive them in the now. Be in gratitude to the people around you for their courage, unknowing though they may be, in acting out conflicts for you.

When I feel someone has done me wrong, I ask myself, when I remember to, "What is my judgment on this person? What have I transferred onto this person or situation from my past? Who do they remind me of, my mom or my dad?"

When I have that answer, the next thing I do is to go into quiet gratitude to the person for showing me the hidden emotional pain from my past, and then I forgive myself, my mom or dad, and whoever else has shown up in my judgments.

Again, by becoming aware of your judgments and emotions and committing yourself to being a player, you can have it all; be at peace with yourself and be part of the change our world so desperately needs. Using the guidelines and tools will ensure you an easy birth into our new paradigm, a world where more and more of us are taking our own healing and transformation seriously and understanding that the only way for our world to change to a more peaceful environment is for us to change to a more peaceful person.

One person at time is the only way. Only you can choose to be a player or a spectator, only you can choose peace instead of war in your daily life. Only you can choose to keep it simple. Only you can choose forgiveness.

Give it a go and witness what happens. Record the results so you can see the difference between when you choose to be a player and when you choose to be a spectator.

⟿ 8 ⟿

When in Doubt, Trust Yourself

THERE HAVE BEEN A FEW KEY TIMES in my life when doubt was not a factor, when not even an ounce of room was given to doubt and the results were lifesaving. In two of the more memorable events, the results were nothing short of miraculous.

Even at the peak of my very successful real estate career, doubt would creep in all the time. Am I ever going to sell another house? Did I do it right? There is no way I can do that again.

In my personal life, doubt creeps in every now and again. It is usually in the form of self-attack. Or feeling like although someone else can do something, I am not like them, and I do not have what it takes.

Doubt is a killer. Yes, a killer! Doubt kills all motivation and keeps us small, a victim to our world, and then a victimizer when we get angry.

A lack of faith in our abilities may be the number one thing that holds us back, often right when we're about to make a breakthrough into happiness, partnership with others, and greater levels of abundance.

The damage done by uncertainty is underestimated; it is a deadly virus in our minds. Insecurity caused by doubting ourselves holds us back and leaves us powerless. The only cure is to stop feeding it and to make another choice.

That's right, when I am in doubt it's because I am choosing doubt, and that is where my energy goes. Wherever I place my attention, the energy grows. So when I think about myself in terms of what I am not and cannot do, doubt grows, and I feel inadequate, nervous, deflated, and scared.

You can make another choice, recognize that you do have what it takes, and trust yourself. One thing that helps me when I find myself in this predicament is a line from A Course in Miracles, "I choose to see this differently."

Writing this chapter has been very interesting. Several examples of doubt have crossed my path, both as personal memories and through friends sharing what had just happened with them. My friends had no idea that my next chapter was about doubt, and it amazed me to have all the stories of lack of faith and insecurity show up in such a timely manner.

Trust Your Instinct

As I mentioned at the start of this chapter, there have been a few times in my life when doubt did not even have a chance to creep in. The first was on an offshore sailing trip in 1982, and the second was during a freeway incident in the early '90s.

I had signed on for the first six months of a round-the-world sailing trip with a family from Vancouver in 1982. It was August when our sailboat left the Fishermen's Wharf at Granville Island in Vancouver. My plan was to go through the Panama Canal and cross the Atlantic with them. There were seven of us on board: the mom, the dad, their three kids, myself, and one other crew. All the youths were the same age, ranging from nineteen to twenty-three.

We spent about a week playing in the Gulf Islands and around Victoria before heading out past Port Angeles. We carried on offshore about one hundred and thirty miles, just outside the shipping lanes. Our destination was San Francisco.

The Oregon Coast is known as one of the heavier weather sailing areas on the globe, and a couple of days into our journey a storm blew up. We were in relatively shallow water for offshore—three hundred miles out would have been a lot deeper and safer.

The wind was blowing at around forty knots, rising at times to over fifty knots. The rain was intense at times. It was night and the sea kept building. Luckily for us, the wind was blowing in the direction we were heading. We hunkered down (and had a triple reef in for those of you familiar with sailing), and reduced the main sail dramatically, leaving a small amount out for a little bit of control. Our fourteen-ton, forty-seven-foot aluminium sailboat was surfing huge waves.

We took two-hour shifts, with two people per shift, and kept rotating throughout the night. It was about three or four o'clock in the morning and Drake and I were on watch next. Being a born salesman, I convinced Drake that there was no way I could handle the boat and talked him into being the helmsman for most of our shift. I promised to make him hot chocolate and get him anything he wanted so I could stay the heck off that wheel.

Finally, about an hour and a half later, Drake said, "I can't take this anymore. I am totally beat. You have to take the helm." I took a deep breath and said okay. I walked through my fear and took charge of our vessel.

Things went surprisingly well at first. I was holding the course at 180 degrees, getting the hang of surfing the waves and feeling empowered. We had fifteen minutes left on our watch when all hell broke loose. Drake was sitting in the cockpit to my right and looking past me to the port side of the boat. He said, "Holy Shit!" and I looked to my left. There was a wall of water so high it must have been forty feet—a rogue wave. Wham! We went down.

The wave knocked us on our side and Drake and I climbed over each other, grabbing at the big hydraulic steering wheel. We hauled on it as hard as we could, but we were going over onto our side into the trough of the wave we had been surfing. We hung on, determined to bring her back, and slowly the boat came around and righted herself. Once we knew we were in control, I started surfing again. There had been no room for doubt, and my reaction was natural, fast, and effective. The only choice I'd had was to trust myself and go for it with all I had. It worked!

When I talk about trusting myself, I am talking about trusting the truth of who I am, not trusting my ego or the self-destructive part of who I am.

We made it safely into San Francisco and the journey continued. There were several more times that, had I chosen doubt, it would have been a disaster, so thank God I was a natural at trusting my true self when it really counted.

After six months, I left the boat and travelled through Costa Rica and Central America before heading back home. The family I was sailing with eventually circumnavigated the globe over the next ten years, ending with only one of their sons on board. Their other son and daughter left the voyage in different parts of the world and took their next steps in life.

The second incident when I did not allow doubt to creep in was in the early '90s. My friend Michael and I were on our way home from Portland after partying all weekend. We were on a freeway in Oregon, hung over, tired, with an eight-hour drive ahead of us. We were speeding along the three-lane freeway when, all of a sudden, all the cars in front of us started to crash into each other. It was mayhem on all lanes, cars going everywhere, hitting each other, braking, and skidding. It was wild.

We were going so fast there was no way to stop our little sports car. I was the passenger. We had a minivan tight on our tail, and he was not stopping either. Something took me over, everything went into slow motion, and I started giving my friend Michael instructions: right, left, brake, gas. We weaved our way through the mess with the minivan hot on our tracks, trusting our moves. I have no idea how we and that minivan made it through, but one thing's for sure, I trusted myself. There was no room for doubt, and we came out the other end intact. The traffic behind us had ground into one big mess, but we had made it through without a scratch.

We have so much assistance from our higher minds when we move on past doubt and trust ourselves. We have a tremendous capacity to receive help and guidance and even miracles when we take a chance and believe in ourselves. The instinctive self is the self I am talking about trusting when I say, "When in Doubt, Trust Yourself!"

My friend Jim is an avid golfer and plays two or three times a week, virtually year round. He was playing with one of his golf pro buddies one day and noticed that the pro was asking for second opinions on the putting green. The first time was from one of the other guys in their foursome, and the second time on the next hole from Jim.

Jim was amazed that the pro was not trusting himself and was succumbing to doubt. No wonder the pro had a tough game, missed his putts in both cases, and was way off his center. When we choose doubt and lose trust in ourselves, defeat is a typical result.

Is it not time to make a different choice? Walk through your fear, throw doubt aside, and trust yourself?

This morning a fitting quote of the day for this chapter arrived by email. The quote is from Don Shula, former NFL coach: "The start is what stops most people."

There may be a few reasons why we do not start or take the next step in our lives, or show up and take a chance and share ourselves with others, yet my belief is the number one reason just may be doubt!

Are you going to choose doubt, or take the next step and commit to playing a new game?

Are you going to keep feeding the doubt in your mind? Are you going to play The Miracle of Change as a spectator and choose the rougher, tougher route in your life, always getting what you have always gotten over and over and over again? Or, are you willing to take the next step, take a chance, choose to be a player and share yourself with others?

It's your choice. Remember, write down your results when you're a player and when you are a spectator, and feel which brings you more ease, happiness, health, and abundance.

Soon you will see, there is a better way, and from there you can trust yourself!

Part Three

You do not need to be wholly willing to change, forgive, or let go of the past—you just need to prefer to.

⌐ 9 ⌐

There May Be No
Second Chance

I T IS MY BELIEF THAT humanity is at a crossroads. We are in a time of great change, a time of choice, as well as a time to celebrate the possibilities.

The crossroads we are at has two directions: the less-travelled path that leads to a better way to live for our-selves, our families, our friends, and our communities, or the highway trod by those who believe they are helpless victims or victimizers.

We have to decide—the easy way or the hard way? Peace or war? Love or fear? Include ourselves or withdraw?

We are at a pivotal time. Do we choose to do nothing and rough it out with what is painful but familiar, or join mil-lions of others on their walk toward a more peaceful planet?

There may be no second chance to make that deci-sion. Do you want to heal your wounds and become part of the positive change that is happening, or will you feed the problems and fears in our world?

I was on the phone the other day with one of my trainer friends talking about how resistance to change is showing up in our world. I believe that if I am aware of something that is happening outside of me, then whatever I've noticed is also in my conscious, subconscious, or unconscious mind. So, if I was noticing resistance to change in others, I must have some resistance myself.

My friend said, "Change or Die Dougie," and hung up the phone. I smiled to myself and thought, *What a friend, and what a great way for her to get her point across.*

When we pull back and forget to forgive, to share of ourselves, to care about others, and to love, we create suffering for ourselves and those around us. Our health and wellness levels drop, life gets harder and more complicated, and generally we are in an unhappy state of mind. When we ignore The Miracle of Change game guidelines and tools we are dangerous to ourselves and others and add negativity to our world.

I believe that in the near future there will be enough people on our planet choosing peace that a whole new Earth will unfold, and that these people will lead the way for our future generations.

Choosing not to be a player in life leads to hardship and unhappiness. You may take yourself off the planet through ill health or accident, or have a very rough ride generally. If you want a healthier, more peaceful, more prosperous future, then choose to be a player, choose forgiveness and peace today.

I have no idea what the new world will look like, but the energy that is propelling the shift to a more peaceful planet has tremendous joy and grace.

21st Century Dynamics Ltd.—Trusting the Process

It was 2004, life was good, my career was booming. I had a sailboat at the marina, a dream cottage on the waterfront, and a convertible BMW in the garage. I had made it back to a very comfortable lifestyle, this time without all the debt.

It was summer and I was lying out on the deck when I received a vision about a company I was to start called 21st Century Dynamics Ltd. It was to become a business coaching and leadership training company. I asked my higher mind to give me a sign when the time was right to take this next step. It would be two-and-a-half years before the call came in, and when it did, things happened fast!

In late February of 2007, I had just returned from more than two months camping in Mexico and was settling back into work as a realtor when the call came. I was walking out of my office to the back parking area. On the way, I passed by our New Listing board where we posted our new real estate listings so we all saw them before they hit the multiple listing service and became public knowledge.

I noticed a new listing and thought nothing of it until I put my hand on the door leading to the parking lot. "Go back and look at the address of that new listing and drive by." The command was unmistakable, and one of the few times I have received such clear instructions from my higher mind.

I drove by, thought it looked all right—country setting, revenue cottage detached from the house, large property, central location—and drove off. I went to Vancouver for a few days on some training and forgot all about the message and the house.

A few days after my return to Sechelt, I asked the listing agent if his new listing was still available. It was, and the circumstances around the sale had prevented the home from being shown. I thought I should at least look at it, but I was very happy in my waterfront cottage, and had no plans whatsoever to move!

I had a look at the property the next day and did not like it at all. Fortunately, I had planned to have lunch with a friend on this same day, and we ended up talking about this home. My friend suggested that since the message to check it out had come from my higher mind, I should reconsider and not dismiss the whole thing altogether.

Long story short, I ended up buying the home despite a competing offer. My offer was lower than the other by a large amount, although I was offering over the asking price, and still the house was mine.

Four days later I got it—this was my call. This was my call to leave real estate and start my new career in business coaching and leadership training. The move would take me out of debt and give me rental income and a home office.

My offer to buy the house was accepted on March 4th, and by March 30th I had sold my twenty-two-year real estate practice, and resigned from a fifteen-year commitment to the board of directors of our larger operation, nine years as chairman. In less than thirty days, I was no longer a realtor, my other professional duties were gone, and I owned two houses.

The miracles came fast and furious. An unexpected windfall from some stock I owned and had no idea would pay off so well was a great help. People showed up with signposts as to where my training may come from, and my mom entered the last year of her life.

This was my chance to be part of the global transformation to world peace. Who knows what my life would be now if I had ignored the call and stayed on the path of my successful real estate career? But one thing is for sure, the past five years have been a huge, accelerated healing time for me—letting go of past pains, hurts, and misunderstandings, and opening my heart.

I had never dreamed that life could be as easy, abundant, happy, fulfilling, loving, and fun as the life that is unfolding for me every day. It just keeps getting better as I choose forgiveness, love, and sharing myself and my gifts. I am grateful that I listened and followed my inner guidance system.

Opportunities come along all the time, and it's up to me to see them. It may be a long time before some of our opportunities come by again, and there may be no second chance.

Do you want to stay as you are, or do you want to step up and start playing the game of your life? Are you ready to open up to your own high capacity for happiness, abundance, and sharing your gifts? The choice is yours—no one else can decide for you.

If it's going to be, it's up to me! Choose to be a player for change and join the millions who understand that there just may be no second chance.

Wisdom Story

Once, a man was passing an elephant when he suddenly stopped, confused by the fact that this huge creature was being held by only a small rope tied to its front leg. No chains, no cage. It was obvious that the elephant could, at any time, break away from that bond, but for some reason it did not.

The man saw a trainer nearby and asked why the animal just stood there and made no attempt to get away. "Well," the trainer said, "when they are very young and much smaller, we use the same size rope to tie them and at that age it's enough to hold them. As they grow up, they are conditioned to believe they cannot break away. They believe the rope can still hold them, so they never try to break free."

The man was amazed. These animals could at any time break free from their bonds, but because they believed they couldn't they were stuck right where they were.

Like the elephants, how many of us go through life hanging onto a belief that we cannot do something, simply because we failed at it once before?

Realize your potential, come out of your old beliefs and the fear of failures. Just because you couldn't do something at one time, or something didn't work earlier, doesn't mean you won't be able to do it now.

—Author Unknown

Our world has everything in it for a life of ease and grace, if we are only willing to heal the past and open up to the possibility of happiness.

⤙ 10 ⤚

When One World Collides
with Another

L IFE IS CHANGING RAPIDLY THESE days, and
some of us are riding the waves of change with ease,
curiosity, and trust. Many people feel as though they're
being pushed around, while still others are being crushed.

Surfing is a great metaphor for what is happening. If
you have ever been to a beach where there are big waves,
you've seen surfers riding the waves, being pushed out of
control by them, or even being crushed into the sand.

Let's talk about being crushed. When life is full of
seemingly insurmountable challenges that could take
you out financially, physically, emotionally, or all three,
it feels like you're being crushed by the waves of change.
Remember, no matter what is happening in our lives, at
some level in our mind we have chosen it this way, and
there's always another choice.

In Hawaii and Mexico I have witnessed surfers, seemingly crushed by a wave, miraculously reappear in the
groove and surf it out. How do they do that? They make a
choice to stay on the board and stay with the wave. They
find a way through their challenge, recover brilliantly,

and have a successful ride. I've also seen surfers go down, but in most cases they brush themselves off and get back out there, unwilling to let the waves beat them.

Being pushed by the waves of change is a little different from being crushed. When I am pushed, I know there has to be a better way, yet I am resistant and fight change all the way to the beach. In a lot of cases, I end up drinking the wave (getting the wind knocked out of me and sucking in water instead of air), which is awful. A few times when body surfing in Hawaii, I drank the wave, and felt like I was going to die. I made it to shore, but it was messy! Other times I have caught the wave and had a thrilling ride, been happy, and laughed lots, eager to get right back out there and do it again.

These days we are being asked, if we are willing, to get out there in our lives and surf the waves of change at home, work, and play. Drink a few, get crushed, recover, and keep getting back out there.

Micro Versus Macro

I love to use the analogy of micro versus macro. Both show us the hologram of our personal lives. Macro is the big picture happening around us in our families, communities, and on the planet. The micro is what is happening in our personal lives. The easy way to have a good look at what is going on inside your mind is to look at the world around you. The outside world is a reflection of your inner world—this is called transference.

For example, when I have a judgment or a negative reaction to someone in my world, it is my old pain I am actually bumping up against—it really has nothing to do with the person who appears to be causing me discomfort. A few years ago, I had major judgments on a high-profile politician. In a POV workshop, I was encouraged to see this judgment as the macro part of my world, and pull it back to myself, the micro, and have a look at where I was running similar patterns in my life. As I did this, and accepted that I was being and doing the very things I was judging, I forgave myself, felt through my emotions, and miraculously I no longer had judgments on that person. I still was not in agreement with all the things he was doing, yet I had a new appreciation that he was doing the best he could with what he had, and I could accept that.

The understanding and acceptance that everything happening outside of us is transference is the ultimate goal and the ultimate prize. This is the big one! When you can accept that transference is playing out in your life every second, twenty-four hours a day, seven days a week, you will have rewarded yourself with one of life's best-kept secrets.

We are in the middle of a paradigm shift here on the planet—what no longer serves us comes up to the surface to be healed. We can get very confused about the reason for all the challenges in peoples' lives right now, but really all that is happening is a sort of cleansing, or detoxing, of our minds. So, the cleansing remedy is the game guidelines, tools, and questions in The Miracle of Change. It's up to you to use them in your daily life with the challenges at hand and make this shift easier for yourself.

Looking at our world and seeing that the old ways of competition, greed, and separation are diminishing, and have never truly served us, will help empower us to choose positive change. Whenever I have experienced what I considered a major shift for the better in my life, I first went through times that were tough, dark, and challenging. My kidney transplant is one example where I was unwilling to

see that there may be another point of view worth consid-
ering. Remember, I shared earlier in this book about having
no plans for transplant or dialysis, as I had convinced myself
that holistic or alternative healing methods could save my
kidneys. I was caught up in the fear of the unknown—what
if I had to have a transplant, what would my life be like
then? I had convinced myself that I would be worse off after
having the transplant than I would be staying the course
and continuing to try to use less intrusive ways to heal.

After I finally agreed to accept my sister's offer of a
kidney, and had the transplant, I was surprised to find
that my life became happier, healthier, and more abundant than ever. As you go about your daily life, be willing
to see that there may be another point of view worth con-
sidering. Look at the world at large, through the news and
through the relationships, actions, beliefs, and thoughts
of those around you. Try to see these as the macro part of
your mind. As you can, pull them back in and have a look
at where these same types of situations, emotions, and
feelings are happening in your life, the micro. In the situations you would like to change, choose a game guideline
and tool from this book and experience for yourself what
happens next.

Another Life Push

Another time of great change for me was in 1995. I had
recovered from the financial disasters of 1991 and yet
had not fully grasped the lesson. At some level, I was still
heavily attached to my material world, but my higher
mind had other plans for me.

Having to sell my beautiful riverfront home and
most of my belongings to cover debts was brutal. I had to
depend on friends for the basics and was terrified of what

would happen next. I had been so successful, worked so hard for ten years, built up an amazing real estate career, and now—devastation. I had no idea that the calamity had been avoidable, the disaster was my own creation, and I had done a bang up job.

Little did I know that my life was about to take a huge turn for the better. Better? Yes, better! A few months passed by, and it occurred to me to ask myself the question, "If money was no object, what would I be doing?" Within a few days, I had an answer, "You will be living and working in a retirement and resort area within two hours of Vancouver." I asked when and what I would be doing there, but the voice gave no response. It is another of the few times the voice from my guides has been loud and clear. Choosing to ask the question, and to trust in a higher power, turned my life around.

Several months later, in February 1996, I was in my Vancouver office when the phone rang and a business colleague offered me an opportunity to market a large condominium project in Sechelt, which is a forty-minute ferry ride from West Vancouver. I immediately remembered what the voice had said, "You will be living and working in a retirement and resort area within two hours of Vancouver." Sechelt fit the bill. I said yes and moved in the next week.

I decided to be a player in the game that is my life. The result was that I rebuilt my real estate career very quickly in this new community, my health and happiness levels went way up, and I had the resources to retire in 2007 to go in this direction of coaching, training, and now writing.

As I've said, and at some level everyone knows, we are in a time of great change. The world based on fear is colliding with the emerging world based on love. When I am surfing the waves of this great change, I am experiencing being a player; when I feel like I'm being pushed around and not in control, I am choosing to be a player only some of the time; when I'm being crushed, I have chosen to be a spectator and to stay in fear.

It's all about choice. Am I going to be a player or a spectator? Am I going to surf these waves of change or be tossed around, or worse, crushed? Do I want to make life easy for myself and those around me, or do I want to make it tough or downright miserable? The game guidelines and tools in this book are there to provide a positive option for every interaction you have, so that eventually choosing love will be automatic.

And the results will stun you.

Surrender

I had no idea what my life would be like when faced with great changes, and yet when I surrendered and accepted that what was happening was in my highest and best interest, or when I just plain surrendered and went through the process, my life became, in all cases, so much easier, richer, and more abundant.

No matter what your challenge, commit to being a player and open to a much happier and more plentiful life.

My darkest and most challenging hours have been followed by the most beautiful and amazing changes that I could ever have imagined.

The Miracle of Change will show you how your thinking affects your life. Be willing, accept that there has to be a better way. Forgive, love, and share yourself and your gifts with those around you.

⟐ 11 ⟐

God (Love) Trumps All

IT WAS 1989, I WAS twenty-nine and walking out of my home to go to work on a mild winter morning. I had a decision to make: Which car to take? Would it be my brand new Mercedes, or the Jeep Grand Cherokee? It was raining slightly, so perhaps the Jeep would be better as I did not like to get the Benz wet if possible, unless it was being washed.

In the midst of this seemingly enviable dilemma, I was unexpectedly and totally overcome with sadness. In a moment of frightening clarity I saw myself, caught up in my material world to the extent that what I owned had become who I was, my things had become my identity. Who was I, really? My whole being knew then that there had to be another way. There had to be a better way. My soul was crying out to me.

For the second time since 1987, something deep inside me was pushing to find God. I know, "Shhhh, not the God word." But God is my word for love. I was aching to find love, to open up to a part of myself that was crying out for help.

I had no idea who I was other than this successful realtor with a fucked up social life and lots of material possessions. I had a family that I did not fully accept and understand and was at odds with most of the time. My family and I got along okay, but that was that, no heart-to-heart chats, the usual niceties while all the underlying hurts from the past shadowed our conversations.

I was waking up, finally hearing something that was calling me from deep within, something so profound that it could get through all the buried pain, blocked emotions, and stubborn beliefs to surface in my conscious mind.

Looking back, I understand that I had finally had enough unhappiness and meaninglessness in my life that I could hear God from deep within me. There was something different inside me, a feeling that I can identify now as love, or God, calling my name and cheering me on.

In my training and coaching, I find that some people are okay with the word God and others cringe or have a negative feeling about it. Some people have no relationship with the word God, while others absolutely reject the concept of God outright. I accept all of these responses, not good or bad, not right or wrong, just as they are!

English is the only language I know, and among English speakers and writers it is my observation that there are many ideas, understandings, misunderstandings, beliefs, and thoughts about what God is, what the word God means, and the definition of God.

For me, God represents a Universal Field of Love, and I don't get caught up in definitions. Whether this Universal Field of Love is called Heaven, Higher Mind, Buddha, the Tao, or whatever else, the name is irrelevant to me. What matters is, does the person, teaching, or program align with love? Does it take me in the direction of love? Is it the road to love? That is what matters to me and to my heart.

Understand with Your Heart

Aside from definitions, there is another great trap on the road to love. Getting caught up in thinking and analyzing teachings that are beyond our understanding instead of feeling and trusting intuition will lead us to reject information that could help change us for the better. Demanding proof that an idea, thought, or word may help before taking a step in a new direction or into new territory leads to always getting what we always had—here we can stay stuck for a long time. As the saying goes, do you want to be right, or happy? Take the chance, try on this new idea, thought, or concept and see for yourself what the results are.

Holding on to beliefs that fuel competition and separation blocks our willingness to change, and we can keep ourselves stuck in a vicious cycle of fear and painful situations. It is here in these fear-based thoughts and beliefs that we typically choose to drink, do drugs, stay super busy, and do all the right things for the wrong reasons.

We have become nice, dead people attached to a world that is quickly disappearing. The world as we know it is dissolving and transforming into the new love-based paradigm. Do you really want to be left behind?

Can you feel that little something deep inside calling out to you—a knowing that there must be another way, a better way? Can you not see that all the busy running around and attachment to the material dream is not meeting your deepest needs?

Material happiness alone is fleeting. No matter how many things we accumulate, our problems and challenges are still with us. Filling the holes in our hearts with cars and houses and status symbols is an act of desperation because the initial feeling of joy or happiness evaporates fast, followed by a need for more. The new of yesterday becomes old hat, and the pattern repeats. We may think we are more comfortable physically but what about how we are feeling?

I am not saying it is bad to have stuff and have goals and aspirations for material things. What I am sharing is that attachment to things is what creates a disconnect from our hearts.

Abundance is our God or Universe-given right, as a child of God or of the Universe we are entitled to all good things. As we align ourselves in this new paradigm, we naturally will share and receive all good things that life has to offer us. We will naturally have the material and financial wellbeing that serves our highest and best interests to continue to heal and transform what is fear-based in our lives; then we naturally align with the truth of who we are and we can be of service to others.

The test for truth in my life is this question: Is this love or fear? For me, love is the truth.

Follow the Love

We become entrenched in an old world of recycling emotions and fear played out in countless stories throughout our lives. If you have a look, you just may find that patterns similar to yours have been playing out for generations, right through your ancestral chain. You can trip the trap, make another choice, choose to know the truth and use the guidelines, tools, and questions given to you in this book.

Don't be fooled by the thought that if you give up everything materially and live a very basic, simple life, all hardships and challenges will go away. Fear-based thoughts and beliefs are still there whether you choose material comforts or not. What we do on the outside will not bring lasting change; it is what we shift on the inside that creates a permanent difference. And by recognizing that the people around us mirror what we need to heal and forgive within ourselves, we can create lasting change.

What if we choose to get curious about what God means to us as individuals? How does God feel to me? What is God? Ask your higher mind to show you; let past perceptions of the word God go and just be curious. Ask yourself, "What does God mean to me?" I encourage you to consider that any meaning or feeling that arises that is not love when you are asking about God is not the truth. The only truth about God is love!

I encourage you to take action and play the game of your life with all your heart. Using The Miracle of Change game guidelines and tools will teach you how to fill your heart with love, and to heal those problems that kept you emotionally and spiritually hungry. Share yourself and give others space to share themselves. Be detached from what you or anyone else thinks about the word God. Just be curious and keep asking your higher mind to show you.

If you have a scientific mind and going into the unknown is difficult for you, check out Gregg Braden, the author of *The God Code*. His research and sharing may assist you to learn to love in a whole new way and to break into abundance and creativity in your life.

Love is what life is all about. Learn what love is, and you are well on your way to healing past pain as it comes up. You are well on your way to forgiving yourself and others when you remember that love is who you are. You are well on your way to aligning with the new Earth paradigm that is unfolding as you read these words. You are well on your way to a happier, more peaceful, more abundant, and healthier life.

Today is the only day you have—are you going to choose to be a player or spectator? Be a player. Be a game changer.

It's Just a Game, and It's All Perfect

T HERE ARE TIMES IN MY LIFE WHEN I just plain forget that life is meant to be easy and abundant, and then there are times when I remember The Miracle of Change philosophy, and am willing to shift or change whatever it is within me that takes me out of the place of ease and flow.

When things are going well, it's a lot easier to look at life in a more carefree way. For the most part, we go on autopilot and just enjoy being happy, healthy, and successful with little thought of how we got here. More importantly, we forget all about giving gratitude to the part of ourselves that resonates in this place all the time.

When to Ask for Help

When our lives are challenging or times get rough, we are more prone to look for, and ask for, help. Learning to ask in the right places can be a game changer.

The first place I go, when I remember, is the emotional component to my problem. I look for and feel into what is bothering me—what is the underlying feeling to what is happening on the surface? I look for what trapped emotion is trying to get my attention. I can usually drop into these emotions as I surrender and trust my process. Second, I ask God, Heaven, my guides, and angels for help. Third, if I feel I need extra help, I ask for coaching in this emotional intelligence and emotional maturity realm. I also ask for help through my coach or a fellow trainer. Psychology of Vision provides lots of support. Their motto is "friends helping friends." When I feel I need a doctor, energy healing, massage, or other health care professionals, I go there next. I am willing to have it all and take the fastest, easiest route back to my happiness; I'll use all of the above together when I need to.

The more I heal and free myself from past pains, hurts, and misunderstandings, the more I see that life is really just a game. We play it constantly and we have waking dreams and sleeping dreams. Now I have you thinking, don't I? If this is plugging you in a little, trust it!

You are about to discover an easy way to shift into a happy, healthy, and abundant you, if you just play along. After all, it's just a game. What have you got to lose? What have you got to gain? Are you willing to step out of your comfort zone, for your own sake and the sake of those you care about?

How to Change Lanes

Looking at life as a game gives me a great advantage, it gives me leverage to look at new ways to enjoy this game and ultimately be a much happier guy. Have you heard the saying, "Change your mind, change your world?" What I am leading you into here is a possible way to change your mind and therefore change your life and your world. I am sharing the "how to" part of the game!

First of all, choose to be a player, and you will see for yourself how this game of life can be played to everyone's advantage. Use this book as a guide to letting go of the past and painful emotions as they come up, and meeting the world with an open heart and forgiving and loving the people around you.

Choose to let go of the past by surrendering to what is happening in your life right now. Trusting your process, forgiving, and feeling through your emotions is guaranteed to put the joy back into living and to attract success on all levels.

As Marianne Williamson puts it, "Spiritual work is not easy. It means the willingness to surrender feelings that seem, while we're in them, like our defense against a greater pain. It means we surrender to God our perceptions of all things."

I interpret the last part as, "Surrender to Love my perceptions of all things," and I use forgiveness and gratitude to help the process as it unfolds.

Gratitude to those around us who act out the subconscious and unconscious parts of our minds for us in living color is another key component to being a player. Remember, right now the idea is to look at yourself and your life as a part of a universal game that is being played out while you are on this planet. When you choose to align with the game guidelines and tools in this book, you will have the opportunity to experience miraculous results, perhaps lasting for the rest of your life.

Einstein said, "You cannot solve a problem with the same mind that created it."

Change your mind through forgiveness and gratitude, and thus dissolve the judgment, anger, and resentment you've stored for so long.

We unknowingly create limitations by ignoring our wounds; now you can free yourself from those chains. Jump off that imaginary cliff and trust that there is and will always be a safety net there to catch you. You will be carried into this new paradigm with ease, grace, and miracles all the way!

The perfect side of the game we are playing and have been playing for our whole lives is that there are no mistakes. Yes, it's my belief that there are no coincidences and there are no mistakes. Everything that has happened to me in my life has been perfect, all the good things, bad things, wins, falls, hardships, misunderstandings, abuses and abusers, all have been part of the perfect plan for my life.

It's all Good—and Here's Why

Remember, everything that has happened and will happen is in our highest and best interests, designed for us to learn to choose a more peaceful, happier way so that we will enjoy ourselves and the people around us that much more. When we share ourselves and our gifts with others, then they, too, can free themselves.

When we accept that there are no mistakes or coincidences, we can look at our life as a platform to heal and forgive ourselves and everyone else—past, present, and future. Since it all has been, is, and will be perfect, we are now free. What no longer serves us will show up for healing and forgiveness. It's all perfect!

When we choose gratitude for the person or situation that is playing out in our lives so that we can heal and free ourselves from a negative emotion, we can forgive and let go. Gratitude alone is one of the most powerful game changers; it may just catapult you forward into ease, flow, and abundance so fast your head spins!

One of the more memorable shifts and healing so far for me has been in my relationship with my family. Healing the pain of past misunderstandings and hurts within my core family has freed me to love them all unconditionally and to appreciate them for who they are with no attachment to their decisions, feedback, or actions—a miracle that has changed my life forever. The game of life is so much easier for me now.

Past stuff still comes up, but I am much more tuned-in, so I acknowledge another layer of past pain that is up for healing and that is that. No need for drama, blaming, fights, misunderstandings, and family feuds.

There are many chapters in this book that can free you from your past, and allow you to enhance the quality of your life and the lives of those around you, yet this chapter is one of the most important. It's just a game, and it's all perfect!

Play like you have nothing to lose. Let go and know that the circumstances in your life are designed to give you a chance to free yourself from all your past pains, hurts, and misunderstandings through forgiveness and gratitude. Once you get the hang of choosing love and forgiveness, you can walk into the future a free woman or man, enjoying life to its fullest and making a difference here on our great planet Earth. Make a difference for the better. Make a difference resonating in peace.

Part Four

Here are paths open to me that have never been opened up before in history. This territory is raw. It is uncharted; it is wide open to a journey of the mind and soul. Where others explored and mapped out the territories of land, it is my task of my era to explore and map out the territories of the mind and spirit. Modern Man is in a unique position to undertake a new journey.

—Sam Keen

☞ 13 ☜

The Paradigm Shift

IT IS SO FITTING THAT ON THE MORNING of Earth Day 2012, I find myself at my computer writing about the paradigm shift that is happening within each and every person on our planet and within Mother Earth herself. My plan for happiness today was to have an Epsom salt bath, do some gardening, and head down to the Roberts Creek Pier and join in the festivities of Earth Day here on the lower Sunshine Coast!

Yet, inside me was a burning desire to write this chapter and have it be part of my contribution to Earth Day 2012. If I can help myself and others to learn to love and respect ourselves, we will naturally respect and love Mother Earth, and she will respond.

My belief is that it matters not how much we try to go out there and fix something that isn't working, or change something for the better, until we recognize why it's broken. If we want lasting change that resonates with love, peace, and the wellbeing of all concerned, we need to find the blocks to that change within ourselves and let them go, through a healing process of acceptance, feeling our emotions, and forgiveness.

We can try to heal our hurts and the planet's, but unless we remove the cause, the drama of hardships and misunderstandings will remain. I am not saying that there is anything wrong with recycling, driving an alternative energy vehicle, or going green, not at all. What I am saying is we will not be able to fix the effects of harming the planet until we find and heal the emotion behind the abuse.

Love and Surrender

Let's take a look at the war on drugs or the war on cancer. Many people head out to fight for change in some aspect of our world, yet do they consider first what is at the root of the problem? What is at the heart of the issue? How to find and change the cause? I am just asking the questions.

Have a look out into the world. When we fight something, it grows, and fear is the paradigm. When we love something, it grows, and we experience peace and miracles and love is the paradigm.

When we surrender rather than fight, inspiration, creativity, and guidance come in to show us a new way. Fighting has fear-based energy; surrender has loved-based energy. I am guiding you to surrender and to be discerning at the same time. Yes, I agree, this is new territory, and your mind may be feeling challenged right now. Just keep forgiving anything that is fear-based and see what happens.

Whether you desire a more positive way of being for yourself or for others, start with love, and experience the difference for yourself.

Looking at issues through the lens of cause and effect, we see that by altering a cause the effect has to change; remove the cause and the issue goes away.

I believe it is possible to have a physical and social environment that supports all life on all levels on our whole planet in a more balanced way. I believe it is possible to create a world of contentment, happiness, clean water, and an abundance of food for all by changing how we think.

When we choose to forgive and we choose love and peace, we feed those feelings into Mother Earth. When we choose fear and anger, we feed those emotions and feelings into Mother Earth. Mother Earth responds to both as cause and effect. Love has the positive effect you'd expect and the negative emotions produce turmoil and destruction.

You ask if I am saying that every thought, every feeling or emotion we all have goes into the emotional energy grid here on Earth? Yes, that is what I am saying. So by forgiving yourself and those around you, you are choosing to be a player, you are feeding love into the grid to the benefit of all. When we forget and make someone else wrong, or fight, or run negative thoughts and energy, we are feeding fear into the grid, to the detriment of all.

What do you want to feed into the grid of our planet? Love, or fear? It is that simple. By choosing to feed love into the grid, you will be naturally aligning with our new paradigm and you will be assisted in miraculous ways. You will be a change agent for peace and will be one of the souls and saints that helps create an easier rebirth for us all.

In celebration of the purpose of Earth Day, let's choose to use the game guidelines, tools, and questions in this book to discover the cause of what no longer serves ourselves and the planet. If we are courageous enough and willing to follow these guidelines, we can shift out of negativity in a few simple steps, thus affecting planet Earth in the same way.

The paradigm shift is happening whether or not you see it or believe it. It is happening now, and it is up to you and me to determine how we want to play in this game of life. With every thought, we produce an outcome, for better or for worse. Pay attention and be a player, take control of your mind and therefore your life. It is our choice, and there is no good or bad, there just is.

Choosing peace, however difficult it may be to do at times, is for the best for you and all those around you. Explore this for yourself. Consciously choose to be a spectator and record your results, then consciously choose to be a player and record your results. Soon you will see which brings you more peace, health, happiness, love, and abundance.

Fear Is an Illusion

Fear is entrenched in our old paradigm, and it's such a waste of time. It is a weapon we use against ourselves and against society. The funny thing is, fear is also an illusion, yet it seems so real. Most of us default to fear as a way of being, and the powers that be effectively use fear to control the masses.

Fear is an illusion? Yes, and there are millions of us waking up to this fact. It started in Tunisia in 2011, moved to Egypt, and then spread across the globe.

The message from our youth is, "Enough," and they are committed to the core of who they are to see that message heard across the globe, so that people like you and me will wake up to the truth. The young people have seen that fear is an illusion, that life is just a game, and that we are all here to be change agents for peace.

Which Way Will You Go?

The paradigm shift we are living has been available in the past. Perhaps two thousand years ago, humanity got close to moving the collective consciousness to love from fear, but at the time there were not enough people who understood the opportunity to make it happen. As a result, the illusion of fear was maintained as the paradigm to live by and the planet carried on.

At this time in history, millions of people have heard the invitation and have agreed to play the game of life in a new way. A large number of people are choosing love over fear, and our fear-based societies are transforming to love-based societies worldwide.

Fortunately, millions of people are waking up each day and deciding to search out the causes of discontent within themselves, then electing to love themselves back to happiness, health, and abundance through forgiveness and gratitude.

Every country on the globe is contributing to our emotional transformation. Some areas are acting out our dark sides so we can forgive the darkness within ourselves. When we look for where we play out similar emotions in our own lives, we can choose to forgive ourselves and, thus, we become part of the paradigm shift in a graceful way. Others are showing us what love looks and feels like, and what love in action looks and feels like so that we can remember the truth of who we really are—loving minds and hearts.

There are acts of kindness, courage, love, and caring happening all over our beautiful planet in escalating numbers, and each act is a major catalyst to the alchemy of change. There is no country on this earth that is not showing and experiencing outstanding acts of love and fear. The turmoil is in our highest and best interests, necessary for us to get motivated enough to cement the move to a love-based humanity.

Yes, that's right, the difference has to come from each and every one of us, one person at a time, going within, finding the cause of what is not working in our day-to-day lives and choosing to try a new path, one that will ultimately create lasting positive change.

We have passed the point of no return, and we are going through this paradigm shift whether we like it or not. The question is, do you want it to be an easy rebirth or not? Do you want to be part of the solution? This is the question you really want to ask yourself. Meditate on it, chew on it, contemplate, savor, and then declare, "I want to be part of the solution and be a player aligning with the game guidelines and tools in this book."

Or, declare that you are choosing to be a spectator and take the slow, hard, painful route that slows down the global process and the shift to world peace. What's important is that you come to a conscious decision either way, rather than drifting along in the dark while life happens around you. Let's all choose to be players and make this rebirth an easier one.

When I find myself in fear, I recognize it as an illusion and I forgive it within myself. Sometimes the fear is so strong, all I can do is think, *Who needs my help?* and just pour my love into that person until the fear in me has gone. It is a great way to move through fear, let it go, and return to love.

Love is who we are, love is who I am, love is the only truth. This enveloping, evolving remembering we're experiencing could be said to be a shift to the truth of who we really are.

Enjoy the ride! Be a change agent for peace, and have some fun remembering the truth of who you are. This is just a game, but the stakes are big right now, so let's all give it our best shot!

So for your sake, the sake of the planet, and those you love, adopt The Miracle of Change philosophy and watch your world transform in miraculous ways.

~ 14 ~

Trust Your Journey

TRUST is investing your mind in a positive outcome; the alternative is investing it in fear and negativity. TRUST is one of the great healing principles; there is nothing it cannot heal. It takes a negative or undetermined situation and paradoxically begins to unfold it toward a positive outcome.

—Chuck Spezzano

S O, GIVEN THAT EVERYTHING that happens to and around us is perfect, and it is all happening for our highest and best interests, let's have a look at trust and see just how powerful it can be for us.

Trust allows us to get on with our day with no second-guessing and to take action with confidence that everything will turn out in our highest and best interests. It frees us up by relieving useless worry and burden from our minds. Trust ultimately releases guilt, and that is a huge comfort in itself!

Whenever I find myself in a mind mess of worry, judgment, fear, or self-attack, it bogs me down and holds me hostage. Yes, here I hold myself hostage to negative thoughts and emotions by feeding the fear and staying in judgment and self-attack; this is a dissociated state of mind. What do you think a mind mess creates for me in my life? Happiness or fear? Love or hate? Health or sickness?

Trusting my journey has become a way of life, most of the time, for me. Wow, what a relief. I accept that what is happening is in my highest and best interests. I keep asking my guides and higher mind for support and direction, and I keep feeling into what my body and my world are communicating to me. From there, I can take action and expect the best.

Life gets so easy. Trust removes all the anxiety and feelings of obligation from my daily life. If other cars are driving slowly, I trust that this is in my best interest, perhaps saving me from an accident or a difficult situation or person. Otherwise, I might have sped up and taken risks or, even worse, gotten all caught up in road rage and done something stupid.

Trust and Grow

When we feel that someone or something has hurt or wronged us in some way in the past, we can lose faith in that person or group or situation and decide never to trust them again. Remember that everyone in our lives is acting out our subconscious and unconscious minds for us so that we can heal our buried emotions in an easy and simple way.

Yes, it is that easy. Trust yourself, trust those around you, and trust that all the happenings in your life are for your highest and best interests. Trust, and forgive what appears to be fear and return to the truth of who you are. Love yourself and trust your journey!

Learning about Trust

Until I could get my head around how and why this game of life is really played, that we all have unique gifts to share with the world in our own way, all this "trust your journey" stuff made no sense to me whatsoever.

I thought it was all a bunch of crap. Trust? What the hell? My life is full of grief, hardship, struggle, health issues, and the world is falling apart.

I was caught up in the corruption, greed, war, and abuse around me. I felt defeated by the world's growing health, environmental, and financial issues, and the lack of food, shelter, and water. Look at all the people who have to wait one or two years for operations even in hospitals in Canada. I could fill several pages with all the complaints and negativity that my world was showing me.

I could have stayed trapped, trying my best to make it in a fear-based world, choosing to chase the All Canadian or American Dream. The one with the most stuff wins. What a life. Gather, gather, gather, fight, fight, fight, some good times followed quickly by more negativity and bad news.

From our birth into a family that soon is abusive and indifferent in one way or another, we go to an unhappy midlife where we are successful or not successful, then on to our old age where we face dying and leaving this planet never having known real love and emotional freedom. The old fear-based paradigm creates the same sad lifecycle generation after generation for the majority of people in our world.

Is it not time, I thought, to wake myself up and choose love? To choose to play the game differently and have a positive and peaceful impact on my world? Thank God I chose to see that there had to be a better way and was willing to find it. Trust has been one of the biggest helpers along this shift for me.

When I trust my journey, I see why things are happening the way they are around me, and see why it's all in my highest and best interest.

Trust allows me to explore avenues that I thought were closed to me, and to find new ways to become happier, healthier, and more abundant.

Trust has become a game changer for me and it has created greater ease and flow in my life.

When I trust my inner guidance system, life goes smoothly, I get lots done, and have time for everything and everyone. I let go of what does not feel true for me and align with what feels good in my body. I make decisions based on my feelings and honor that those feelings are guiding me to a happier, healthier, easier way of being.

Trusting my journey is by far an easier way to live. I can know that no matter what, I am in the right place at the right time and all is perfect. I am in a place of healing, which can be uncomfortable, or I am in a place of love, feeling peaceful, and that is that.

Trusting my journey has helped me to open up to more creativity and to find solutions for my life and the lives of others that I never could have dreamed of a few years ago.

Trust is allowing me to see a different world, a beautiful world full of opportunity, abundance, and possibilities. It allows me to see that all things are perfect, even the things that we the people want changed. At the same time, we have to be willing to change ourselves. It is how the game works. Whatever I can see outside of myself is a reflection of what is in me—it is that simple.

When events get dramatic and challenging, unfair or cruel, they are just ramping up so that I cannot miss the lesson, and then I can choose whether I want to respond as a player or a spectator.

Trust your journey. Trust that you are in the perfect place at the perfect time to be a change agent for peace, health, and prosperity.

No matter what your life looks like right now, no matter what is happening, trust with all your willingness and courage that it is perfect for you.

Remember, it's just a game. Choose to be a player, then choose to be a spectator, experience the differences, and then choose the one that brings you the most positive results. Do it for yourself, for those you love, and for the whole world.

～ 15 ～

Courage to Go Beyond
Your Limits

IT WAS 1984, AND A group of friends had set up a day to go skydiving. I counted myself in. I was terrified, yet somehow I walked through it enough to get into the game and head out with them. It was time to bust through one of my greatest fears—heights!

The day unfolded brilliantly. We spent six hours training for the jump and all was fun and went well. After the training, we packed our parachutes and the six of us piled into a little Cessna airplane. We were off. At about three thousand feet, it occurred to me that watching anyone else jump might send me into more fear, so I volunteered to go first.

Oh man, was it fun. I had no idea how thrilling jumping out of a plane could be! I was on top of the world, floating through the air and loving every moment. Even the landing was great. The emotional high lasted for several hours after the jump. We'd all had a great time and took great satisfaction from the fact that we had stretched ourselves beyond our limits.

Beyond the Limits

We are at a pivotal time in our history and no business, organization, group, family, or individual will escape the change. So it is up to us, when we are willing, to gather up the courage to go beyond our limits.

The limits I am talking about are negative perceptions, emotions, thoughts, beliefs, and desires that smother happiness and wellbeing. They cause a lot of grief and hardship and affect our health, wealth, and relationships.

When I am sharing about our perceptions, emotions, thoughts, beliefs, and desires, I am referring to the process I believe our conscious, subconscious, and unconscious minds go through to store our experiences.

It is at the desire level in the unconscious part of our mind where we create lasting change. The easiest way I have discovered so far to access that part of my mind is to start with my perception in my conscious mind, and ask myself, "What is the emotion I am feeling around this?" Then I start to get in touch with my emotions, thoughts, and beliefs in my subconscious mind, and then I drop into my desire in my unconscious mind. Nothing changes until I get to that level and understand what's really going on.

Let's say I am angry at someone close to me, and I feel they have wronged me in some way. My perception is that they have hurt me. Under this is perhaps my emotion of anger, then sadness, and then I discover my thoughts and beliefs. Eventually, I will see that I desire it this way. Usually, I have plugged into past pain and an old grievance that I do not want to give up.

This is just a mistake in our minds, and when we feel we have been hurt, this is when we choose fear instead of sharing our gifts and hearts. At the desire level, we can choose once again to open our hearts and share our gifts—it is not too late. As we share our gifts with those involved in the blame and hurt, we replace the old grief with loving beliefs, thoughts, emotions, and perceptions. From here, our lives have lasting change, as the underlying desire has been changed and we have freed up another part of our mind. Many refer to this as healing or integrating our mind.

What You Can't See Can Hurt You

Most of us are, and have been for some time, dissociated from about 95 percent of our emotional life. What impact do you think it may have when we cannot name 95 percent of what we are feeling, and are completely blind to the impact those feelings have on everything we think and do?

Do you think it is time to free yourself and go beyond your known limits? Ninety-five percent of your freedom is sitting there waiting for you to claim it!

So, in this game of life, why not be the first of your group, family, team, business, or organization to take the jump? Become a player and lead the way through fear with acceptance, forgiveness, and gratitude. Show by example a better way to live.

The Iceberg Model of Awareness

Let's have a look at the following iceberg model. The area above the surface is called our conscious mind, this is the 5 percent of our mind that we are exposed to, just like the part of the iceberg that is exposed to the world above the water's surface.

Below the surface is the remaining 95 percent of our mind, called our subconscious and unconscious.

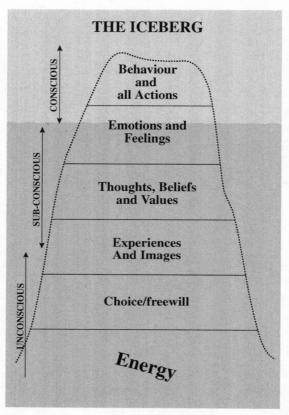

THE ICEBERG

CONSCIOUS

SUB-CONSCIOUS

UNCONSCIOUS

Behaviour and all Actions

Emotions and Feelings

Thoughts, Beliefs and Values

Experiences And Images

Choice/freewill

Energy

I use this iceberg model in my leadership training and coaching very effectively.

From Steps to Leadership, a training program of the Psychology of Vision model created by Chuck and Lency Spezzano. (Published by VisionWorks Life Skills Ltd. UK)

Our perceptions are above the surface, and as you can see, almost all of our thoughts, beliefs, and desires are below the surface, out of our sight. Our desires are in the unconscious part of our mind, in the choice and freewill section of the iceberg.

Letting It Go

The way to change my desires is first to identify the perceptions in my conscious mind, and then trace these to the emotions in my subconscious mind. As I feel the emotions, I focus on the associated thoughts and beliefs stored in the subconscious.

Once I make those connections consciously, I can discover the desires that have been driving me from within my unconscious mind. With that understanding, I am now in a position to create the change that I would like.

When I discover that one of my desires is based in fear, I have an opportunity to turn it into a love-based desire by accepting it, forgiving it, forgiving myself, and letting it go. It is that simple.

For example, recently I found myself in deep fear around a relationship situation and wanting it to be different than it was. I was almost taken out by it. The first thing I did was to feel the fear and ask myself, "What emotion is under this fear?" As I explored my emotions, I could feel sadness and anger, and under that was heartbreak and a feeling of being left out or ignored by my friend. First, I accepted my new discovery, and then I said to myself, "Thank you, I love you." This is one way I use forgiveness.

Throughout this process, I was breathing deeply, allowing the fear to rise up through my body and out the top of my head and letting it go. When I am feeling my emotions, it helps to breathe from the base of my spine or even from my feet, all the way up through my body, and then back down to the base of my spine or feet, whichever feels best. Breathing really helps me to feel and helps my letting go process immensely.

The best news is that every day, the people in our lives are acting out right in front of us the feelings and emotions that we are dissociated from. When we recognize that their actions are reflecting back to us our own perceptions, thoughts, beliefs, and desires, we can slow down and engage with the world on a new level rather than reacting blindly.

As our friends, family, and the world help us to discover our true desires, we can decide to keep them or use The Miracle of Change game guidelines and tools to make a positive difference.

This is not new information, but most people have not yet sought out and used these methods to heal themselves. So now you have the easy way through, to go beyond your current way of thinking, access your subconscious and unconscious, and shine your light on these shadow parts of your mind.

A great way for me to fast track this process is to ask myself, in any situation, "Why do I want it this way?" This is powerful because it reminds me that at some level I am responsible for what is happening. I may be completely dissociated from whatever prompted me to make the choice, but asking the question opens the door to understanding.

Remember that The Miracle of Change game guidelines and tools are at your disposal, so use them wisely and commit to taking control of your mind. Set yourself free!

Freedom Takes Courage

We have become so accustomed to automatically reacting that sometimes setting ourselves free from old habits is challenging. At times, it takes all my courage and willpower to forge ahead one step at a time, asking for help as I need it, and recommitting to the next step toward happiness and the truth of who I am.

All it takes to shift and create positive change is the willingness or preference and courage to go beyond my limited way of thinking. Are you willing to go beyond your limits? Bust through whatever is keeping you unhappy using acceptance, forgiveness, and gratitude? Then reach back and help others who are there waiting for your help. As more and more people choose to start being more accountable and responsible for their lives and to create positive change, the less time it will take to free our planet from this fear-based paradigm.

Communication—the Surprising Reality

Over the past five years, I have come to realize the importance of being aware of the different types of communication we use in our daily interactions.

We communicate verbally, paraverbally, and visually, among other means. I have come to learn, through the Steps to Leadership program I teach, that about 7 percent of all our communication is verbal, 38 percent is paraverbal, and 55 percent is visual. This is the impact, or effectiveness, that each type of communication has in our daily interactions. Verbal communications are the words we speak, while paraverbal communications are the voice tones and sounds that we make other than our words. Visual communications include our actions, body language, movements, and nonverbal expressions.

For the most part, none of this is surprising or even new information, yet when I look at these different types of communication styles, life starts to make more sense and have more meaning. Especially when I pay attention to my own style of communication and become aware of my nonverbal communications!

Do your own experiment. Pay close attention to others' signals and become aware of how your own voice tones and body language reflect your emotions and feelings. They add up to 93 percent of what we are communicating all the time, twenty-four hours a day, seven days a week. This awareness will help you to see and feel what is going on in your subconscious or unconscious mind.

In the intense experiential training I've received over the past five years, I have become aware of how dissociated I was from my feelings and emotions. In the case of the iceberg model, I was perhaps 95 percent dissociated. In the case of my communications, I was at least 55 percent dissociated, and perhaps at times up to 93 percent dissociated.

I am sharing this information with you so it may help you to understand more about how our minds work and how we communicate.

Heavenletter

The following is a message that was shared with me on *SpiritLibrary.com* from April 25, 2012. Some people might find this a stretch. I recommend then to treat it as a meditation and read slowly and breathe deeply as you go.

It doesn't matter whether or not you agree with this information, what matters is that you open your mind enough to ask yourself, "What if?" Allow yourself the opportunity to have the courage to go beyond your limits!

Heavenletter #4168 There Is No Between

a message from God *written down by* Gloria Wendroff
Monday, 23 April, 2012 (posted 25 April, 2012)

Whatever you look at, you are seeing yourself. You are the ocean you look at, and you are the waves, and you are the sky and you are the sand. There is only Oneness, and, yet, you are everything. You are My Everything and Everyone, and, still, We are One.

You are the stars at night, and you are the streetlights. You are the moon, and you are a pot on the stove.

There is nothing you are not, and, yet, Oneness alone is.

That is why you are everything imagined and True Oneness all rolled into One.

You are the traffic, and you are the solitary eagle.

You are the flies and mosquitoes that buzz around.

You are the bees who make honey. You are the caterpillars who change into butterflies. You are man, woman, and child, and you are ascending.

You are the sound of crickets and the TV. You are lips that kiss, and you have a voice that sings and hums as you go about your work.

There is nothing you are not.

You are every wish that ever came true. You are My desires manifested into a between world, a world birthed from Heaven and debated about on Earth. You are a wonder of creation, and you wonder about yourself and what you're up to.

And you are the firmament of love, and you are love taking a chance and brave about it.

You are the sun that rises and the sun that sets.

You are everything, and you are nothing at all.

Your body is a physical representation of a magnificent soul. Whatever the body does or appears like, you are not your body. You are soul. Body is temporary. Soul is always. Body and soul are almost like from two different countries. Your soul is true. Your body is fake.

You are the streams of the river, and you are the bathtub, and you take a bath, and you dry yourself off.

You ponder the state of life you are fantasizing as if you were physically real instead of a thought.

You are a thought, that thought itself.

You are a downspout, and you are an elevator going up.

You are many things. Still, you are One.

You are not My shadow. You are My light, and a spotlight is on you.

There is nothing that stands between Us, and We share love. Our love overlaps.

At first you think it is nonsense when I say you are a downspout, and you are an elevator going up, or that you are the bee who makes honey and so on. Yet something about what I say begins to feel right to you.

Beloveds, there is nothing that you are not, and I alone AM. At first this seems like an exaggeration, yet it is the whole Truth.

There is nothing you are not.

Those you love are you.

Those you do not feel love for are you.

There is nothing really that comes between you and another, another who seems like another and, yet, who is you. You are the other looking at himself but since there is no other, you are looking at you and calling yourself by another name, as if you and the seeming other were not One.

Wherever you look, you are Oneness peering at yourself. Whoever speaks, you are the speaker. Whoever listens, you are the listener. Whoever paints, you are the artist. Whoever

*makes music, it is you. There is no between. There is no
other. There is Oneness. You might as well get used to the
idea, for that is the Truth and nothing else is.*

(From *www.heavenletters.org.*)

Be sure to re-read the last paragraph. For me it says it
all. Forgive the world around me every chance I get—it's
just me!

The many experiential training workshops and the
coaching I have received have stretched me far beyond
what I thought were the limits in my life. My heart has
opened up, I can feel my feelings and emotions, and I
have transformed many close relationships. My daily life
and way of being has changed to a more relaxed yet pro-
ductive lifestyle, and there is more gratitude, freedom,
and happiness.

These have been the toughest five years of my life, as
well as the most rewarding, loving, heartfelt, and joyous,
all wrapped up in a bundle together.

It has taken willingness, courage, and commitment
to go beyond limiting beliefs and thought patterns to
open myself up and be willing to feel my emotions and
feelings. The process has truly helped set me free of emotional wounds that kept me in a state of discontent. The
healing so far has allowed me to open up my heart, intuition, inner guidance, and creativity, and has created a
new ease in life—it has changed my life forever.

I would not have ever dreamed that I would one day
be writing a book, teaching, training, and helping others
in such profound ways. This is truly a dream come true
for me. I am so grateful I have the courage to go beyond
my limits.

ᴄ 16 ᴄ

If Not You, Then Who?

I AM SURE BY NOW YOU ARE STARTING to feel that if you do not take charge of the changes you would like to see in the world and within yourself, no one else can do it for you.

When I say take charge, I really mean make new choices that will lead to the happiness, joy, and love you have been so longing for all your life.

Again you are faced with deciding whether or not to take a step and go further toward the truth of the world and the truth of who you are. If no one else can take this step for you, then what? When you prefer the status quo and avoid change, what happens to you and to the world around you?

The crossroads can feel very challenging, but it is a great place, a place of opportunity. We can stay in the same old rut and keep creating the same old discontented lives, or we can walk a new path into the unknown. One of our greatest fears as humans is the unknown. The possibility of uncovering buried emotions can be frightening, and we can use the fear, and even milk it, just to hold ourselves back.

We use fear to stop ourselves, to create chaos and misunderstandings. We use fear to attack ourselves and

"Thoughts are not big or little, powerful or weak. They are merely true or false." (W-p1-16:1:4-5) Permission granted by The Foundation for Inner Peace, publisher of *A Course in Miracles*.

others, and we use it in such painful and harmful ways that we create lives of hell on earth. When we are stuck in fear, we tend to act out and project our emotional pains and stay dissociated. One of the reasons we do this is that we are afraid of our greatness, of our brightness, and we are afraid to shine.

The great news about fear is that it is an illusion—yes, it is not real. Fear can sure feel real, in fact it can feel bigger than a double-decker bus! Yet, the fact remains that fear is not real.

Fear is a false thought, it is not the truth. The test for truth I use is, "Does this thought align with love?" When it does not feel like love, then I know it is not the truth and therefore it is just an illusion.

Now we come to the "how to" part of this equation. The easiest, most effective way I have found yet to deal with, and walk through, my fear is a practice called Ho'oponopono, saying to myself, "I am sorry, please forgive me, thank you, I love you."

Ho'oponopono has become an automatic response that I use every day, and it helps me move through my fear.

I will share some history and resource information about Ho'oponopono with you in a minute. First, I would like to share a way to use Ho'oponopono in a condensed form that is still very effective in helping to dissolve fear.

When fear comes up, when I have a fear-based thought, or when someone else appears to be making me angry, I try to remember to say to myself, "Thank you, I love you." That's it—"Thank you, I love you." I say this to any and all fear-based thoughts. Remembering that fear is not real helps me to return to a more peaceful place within myself.

Think, "Thank you, I love you." Breathe, then think, "I am sorry for using you to act this out for me so I can see it in myself, please forgive me, thank you, I love you."

I use the words "Thank you, I love you," so much in my daily life with miraculous results. I am grateful for discovering Ho'oponopono. Every time I witness a thought in my mind that is negative, maybe something like, *You are going to get in a car accident*, I say internally *Thank you, I love you*. Immediately, I feel more relaxed and back in a freer state of mind. I was skiing last week, and at the top of one of the steep runs, I had this thought: *What if I wipe out and hurt myself?* I said in my mind, *Thank you,*

I love you, and the fear disappeared. Other times I have used Ho'oponopono to deal with my health, or to handle difficult friendships and relationships. In most cases, the results are nothing short of miraculous!

Test this out in your daily life, see for yourself the results, and then you be the judge of whether it helps you or not. Ho'oponopono is meant to be a feeling, an internal technique, and when used internally it can be miraculous. If you have not experienced using Ho'oponopono yet, give it a try. Thinking "Thank you, I love you" is the easy and effective way to play with it. Ho'oponopono is an ancient Hawaiian practice, and from my understanding this healing modality was brought to us by Hawaiian healer Morrnah Nalamaku Simeona. Later on, the practice was simplified and practically applied by Dr. Ihaleakala Hew Len with absolutely miraculous results.

The book *Zero Limits* by Joe Vitale describes Ho'oponopono. The book is about Dr. Ihaleakala Hew Len, who emptied a ward for mentally insane criminals in a couple of years, just saying a few words to himself. I recommend this book to my clients and students all the time; it is an easy read and a great book.

I encourage you to give Ho'oponopono a try in your daily life and witness for yourself the results.

≈ 17 ≈

The Last Frontier

WELL HERE WE ARE, finally, the whole world faced with the option to journey into the last frontier. Every time I feel into this journey, the last frontier, I cannot help but imagine North America's gold rush days in the 1800s and the hardships those people endured. They showed courage, dedication, and the willingness to do whatever it took to discover gold.

They saw rough times and good times, fights, and natural disasters. There were sad times of defeat and breakthroughs into success, broken friendships and bonds so deep they lasted a lifetime, through thick and thin. I imagine myself back in those times and feel the parallel they have to our current gold rush, to the gold of our last frontier—a journey from our minds to our hearts.

We have come to a crossroads and millions are choosing the last frontier as their path. In the game of life, as in this book, it is the players, not the spectators, who receive the gold at the end of the rainbow. The spectators sit back, judge, criticize, even feel hatred toward the players, and in the end have difficult lives.

Love the People Who Hate Us

An interesting quotation about hatred crossed my desk recently. It said, "Those who hate us want to be like us."

We can either love the people who hate us and trust that they will choose to become players, or we can return their hatred and get sucked back into being a spectator ourselves. Either way, those of us who are on the path into our hearts know that it is love that works in all circumstances. After all, love is truth, and nothing else matters.

When sharing with people my thoughts and feelings about the last frontier, the journey few men and women have dared to take, often the response will be, "Wow, that is deep!" To me, they are saying, "Yes, something deep inside me recognizes that as true, and this is new and uncharted territory." I know then that there has been a shift, and that at some level their heart and soul have cracked open. Now it is just a matter of trust and divine timing. I carry on mentoring and modeling and have no attachment to their choices.

Men and women have searched our planet corner to corner to find their heart's desire. They have spent billions of dollars and billions of hours trying to find happiness and to connect with something meaningful out there somewhere. If only they'd known that what they were searching for was right there inside them all along. As the song says, "Looking for love in all the wrong places."

A friend of mine back in the late '80s, let's call him George, was a perfect example of someone looking for love in all the wrong places. We worked together in the same real estate firm in North Vancouver for several years. George was a moderate producer. He sold enough homes to live comfortably and had disposable income to play with. George was at unrest with himself and was on the hunt for happiness. He would sell a few homes, then book a trip.

Over the years that I knew George, he travelled often, all over the world. He would eventually come back to work, sell a few more homes, and off he went again to another country on another quest to find happiness. One day George walked into my office and sat himself down. He said, "You know Doug, I have travelled all over the world, spent all my money, and I have just realized . . . I am still restless, unhappy, and searching." We both had a good laugh.

God bless you George, thank you for leading the way. Whether you knew it or not, you were modeling and mentoring for the rest of us. Those of us who are paying attention sooner or later figure out that happiness is inside us, and no matter where we travel, unless we make that internal journey, we'll never find what we're looking for.

These days I travel often for work, for adventure, and to spend time with friends. I love it, but I am just as happy at home as I am when I travel. On the flip side, if I am choosing to be unhappy, it does not matter where I am physically on the planet, I am still unhappy.

This awareness is great news—it means happiness is ours for the choosing, anywhere, any time. Happiness is inside us and has been there from our beginning. It is now up to us to embark on our own journey into the last frontier, to go within, open our minds, and build a bridge to our open hearts.

Material Wealth

Another place many of us look for our happiness and love is in our work and businesses. We pour all of our energy into trying to get rich and acquiring status symbols, expecting each new thing will be the one that makes us happy. We're sure that this material gift will save our friendship or marriage or partnership. It's an endless cycle of delusion.

Many of us will go to great lengths to acquire money and hopefully fortunes. We move to new towns, change jobs, change careers, and yet there we are. Soon the new town seems to have all the same issues the last one did; the towns look different, yet the dynamics are the same. At first the new job is great, but soon the people seem to magically develop the same or similar irritating issues as previous colleagues. The scenarios repeat in each new job, career, and town.

All the time that we think we're running toward what we want most in life, we are in fact running away. We are running from the only source of happiness we have—ourselves. When we finally slow down a bit, and stop long enough to consider, we have a chance to find the way that works. Like the 49ers of the gold rush, it takes willingness and courage to enter and explore where few have gone before us. Everything we have been looking for has been right here inside us the whole time. The last frontier!

The following brilliant message is an excerpt from Russell Conwell's book *Acres of Diamonds*. The author delivered this message over five thousand times at various places from 1900–1925.

Acres of Diamonds

When going down the Tigris and Euphrates rivers many years ago with a party of English travelers I found myself under the direction of an old Arab guide whom we hired up at Baghdad, and I have often thought how that guide resembled our barbers in certain mental characteristics. He thought that it was not only his duty to guide us down those rivers, and do what he was paid for doing, but to entertain us with stories curious and weird, ancient and modern, strange and familiar. Many of them I have forgotten, and I am glad I have, but there is one I shall never forget.

The old guide told me that there once lived not far from the River Indus an ancient Persian by the name of Ali Hafed. He said that Ali Hafed owned a very large farm; that he had orchards, grain-fields, and gardens; that he had money at interest and was a wealthy and contented man. One day there visited that old Persian farmer one of those ancient Buddhist priests, one of the wise men of the East.

The old priest told Ali Hafed that if he had one diamond the size of his thumb he could purchase the county, and if he had a mine of diamonds he could place his children upon thrones through the influence of their great wealth. Ali Hafed heard all about diamonds, how much they were worth, and went to his bed that night a poor man. He had not lost anything, but he was poor because he was discontented, and discontented because he feared he was poor. He said, "I want a mine of diamonds," and he lay awake all night. Early in the morning he sought out the priest. I know by experience that a priest is very cross when awakened early in the morning, and when he shook that old priest out of his dreams, Ali Hafed said to him:

"Will you tell me where I find diamonds?"

"Diamonds! What do you want with diamonds?"

"Why, I wish to be immensely rich."

"Well, then, go along and find them. That is all you have to do; go and find them, and then you have them."

"But I don't know where to go."

"Well, if you will find a river that runs through white sands, between high mountains, in those white sands you will always find diamonds."

"I don't believe there is any such river."

"Oh yes, there are plenty of them. All you have to do is to go and find them, and then you have them."

Said Ali Hafed, "I will go."

So he sold his farm, collected his money, left his family in the charge of a neighbor, and away he went in search of diamonds. He began his search, very properly to my mind, at the Mountains of the Moon. Afterward he came around into Palestine, then wandered on into Europe, and at last when his money was all spent and he was in rags, wretchedness, and poverty, he stood on the shore of that bay at Barcelona, in Spain, when a great tidal wave came rolling in between the pillars of Hercules, and the poor, afflicted, suffering, dying man could not resist the awful temptation to cast himself into that incoming tide, and he sank beneath its foaming crest, never to rise in this life again.

The man who had purchased Ali Hafed's farm one day led his camel into the garden to drink, and as that camel put its nose into the shallow water of that garden brook, Ali Hafed's successor noticed a curious flash of light from the white sands of the stream. He pulled out a black stone having an eye of light reflecting all the hues of the rainbow. He took the pebble into the house and put it on the mantel which covers the central fires, and forgot all about it.

A few days later this same old priest came in to visit Ali Hafed's successor, and the moment he opened that drawing-room door he saw that flash of light on the mantel, and he rushed up to it, and shouted:

"Here is a diamond! Has Ali Hafed returned?"

"Oh no, Ali Hafed has not returned, and that is not a diamond. That is nothing but a stone we found right out here in our own garden."

"But," said the priest, "I tell you I know a diamond when I see it. I know positively that is a diamond."

Then together they rushed out into that old garden and stirred up the white sands with their fingers, and lo! There came up other more beautiful and valuable gems than the first. "Thus," said the guide to me, "was discovered the diamond-mine of Golconda, the most magnificent diamond-mine in all the history of mankind, excelling the Kimberly itself. The Kohinoor, and the Orloff of the crown jewels of England and Russia, the largest on earth, came from that mine."

When that old Arab guide told me the second chapter of his story, he then took off his Turkish cap and swung it around in the air again to get my attention to the moral. Those Arab guides have morals to their stories, although they are not always moral. As he swung his hat, he said to me, "Had Ali Hafed remained at home and dug in his own cellar, or underneath his own wheat fields or in his own garden, instead of wretchedness, starvation, and death by suicide in a strange land, he would have had 'acres of diamonds.' For every acre of that old farm, yes, every shovelful, afterward revealed gems which since have decorated the crowns of monarchs."

(From *Acres of Diamonds*. Published by Harper & Brothers, 1915.)

The challenge we face is to find our own acres of diamonds. There may be some rocks and debris to move out of the way, but breech the last frontier and you'll find the treasure of your dreams. Love, kindness, health, abundance, creativity, happiness, and joy—these are riches that last and multiply with time.

It's time to choose your path. Trust your decision and know that no matter what you choose, it will be the perfect choice for you. Just remember, if you are not enjoying the choice you have made, it is your God-given right to choose again. Choose to be a player, and set yourself free into the richness of your mind, heart, and soul.

⇜ 18 ⇝

Before the Dawn

BY NOW YOU HOPEFULLY have been working with the guidelines, tools, and questions set out in this book. It is my belief that humanity is being offered an opportunity to become more peaceful, loving, happy, and abundant. Your willingness to improve your relationships and have a happier life will determine your experience.

That is the good news. Now for the kick-in-the-butt news. Do you want to wait until you are forced into a positive mode as your world changes around you? Or will you be proactive and be an example of how to live the love paradigm from where you are playing right now?

For many people, it has taken a crisis situation to motivate them to consider changing their beliefs, becoming more neighborly, helping friends in need, and, especially, walking toward their original families and committing beyond all else to love them no matter what it takes.

Have a look at the world at large and see it as a macro version of your life. Just play with me here for a bit and see where this takes you. Have a look at the country you live in and now take a good look at the economy, the politics, the job situation, the cost of living, the debt, the price of real estate, the price of cars, the cost of a pair of shoes for a child.

Now look around at your neighboring communities. Has their area been burned-out or flooded? Has the sole industry of any nearby community just closed down? How many people are living in a residence and what rent or mortgage are they paying? Have you noticed more people living on the streets?

In the part of the world where I live, most people are very lucky and still appear to be maintaining a comfortable life, yet when I get inquisitive, it does not take long to understand that they are concerned about their businesses, their jobs, and their ability to pay their debt, let alone retire. Somehow most people are cruising along right now as if all is right with the world, while knowing that the very mesh, the fabric of our society, is rotten and coming undone.

We are holding our breath, so to speak, and many of us are being proactive and finding ways to feel secure no matter what happens. So far, the only true security I have found is in the sanctuary of my own heart. That's right, my own heart. It is my belief that this is what these times are all about. What is it going to take to be willing to open our hearts and know that love and kindness are the only ways we will ever find true security?

There are a few signs to consider that will help show you whether you are truly opening your heart. When your heart is not open, the evidence is all around you, regardless of what your mind is telling you. For example, when you think you have opened your heart and that you are full of love, but your world is full of difficult relationships, scarcity of any sort, irritating people at the store, at work, or at the organization you belong to, and you find yourself judging them, then you have closed your heart.

Not an Easy Journey

Most of us do not even venture on the journey between our heads and our hearts because it can be intimidating! The first thing that tends to happen is that we hit some dark places in our mind—we're afraid to feel the emotions and we back off. We love to go to happy places in our memories and feel all loving and secure, but to be able to truly forgive others and ourselves we have to bring the hard feelings into the light to be understood, accepted, forgiven, and let go.

For most people, when they start to look beneath the surface of their consciousness, subconscious memories of incidents that scarred them start to surface. The pain associated with those memories soon puts an end to the exercise.

The game guidelines and tools in this book teach how to use acceptance to put old wounds into perspective and forgiveness to heal the damage. Once you've mastered the ability to accept what is, forgive, and then move on, you'll be able to lead the way for others, making it easier for those around you to open their hearts and live their life in a more loving way.

Each person's successful journey makes the way easier for others because as you do your healing and transformation, you are no longer projecting the shadow parts of your mind onto the people around you, and they are now reflecting back your true nature. They become happier because they are no longer acting out your negative projections, and you're now living proof that adopting a love paradigm works.

Keep in mind that although your friends and family may notice the positive changes in your interactions, they'll have no clue what is creating the change unless you tell them about The Miracle of Change and how it directs your healing through your own inner journey.

Let The Miracle of Change Guide You

These times are providing all of us the chance to be willing to venture through and heal the negative parts of our minds so we can open our hearts once and for all. The game guidelines, tools, and questions in this book give you an advantage on your journey through the negative parts of your conscious, subconscious, and unconscious, and help make healing possible.

It may be a surprise that all that dark, negative stuff you have buried is more willing to go away than you are willing to let it go. Your conscious mind prefers to keep these negative memories buried in your subconscious because there is a price to pay when you are willing to let them go.

The price is letting other people off the hook. Most people feel that all those people who hurt us deserve punishment in one way or another. It's time to let them off the hook and forgive them unconditionally, or else you will be the one who has the rough life, and it will get a lot rougher if you choose to keep hanging on in the spectator role.

Feel your emotions, forgive, let go, and start enjoying a happier life with a more loving family and closer friendships.

With a settled mind and open heart, you'll experience a connection to your own inner guidance system and a place where you can feel safe no matter what is happening. The alternative is continued fear of what is going to happen next: When is the financial system going to collapse? What about my future? Where are we going to live?

Thousands, if not millions of people are haunted by such questions today.

Services that people in the western world have come to take for granted are deteriorating, and the structures of our societies are weakening. Necessary entities such as hospitals and health care in many countries around the world are overloaded, overworked, and barely meeting people's needs.

By using the guidelines and tools in this book, you can find solutions to your problems, and experience miracles with your health and your health care. Play the game of your life with these guidelines and tools and see for yourself what happens. Again, I am simply suggesting you try it out. What have you got to lose?

Time for Action

I watch people sit around and quibble for hours on end over whether something will work or not, unwilling to just get on with it and give it a go. It is time to get on with it before a crisis hits and offers you only one choice, to play the game or suffer.

This may seem harsh, but we are in times when safely waiting and watching has come to an end. The longer you stay in competition mode, the tougher the next few years will be for you. It is perfectly fine to choose to be a spectator and accept the consequences; that is your right. I am talking to the people who understand that using the guidelines and tools in this book is the way to the life they want but are afraid to commit to doing the emotional clearing that goes with it. I am also acknowledging the people who are being proactive and encouraging others to keep going. They are confirming for the people willing to be the leaders for change in their family, community, and the world that they are all so desperately needed.

This is a wakeup call before the piano falls out of the sky and lands on your head. For those of you who are now in, or recently have been in a crisis, the game guidelines and tools in this book will help you to have an easier recovery and to rebuild your life and the lives around you with an open heart. It is our hearts that matter, nothing else will give us safety.

As you commit and recommit to being a part of the solution and not part of the problem, humanity will rise like a phoenix out of the ashes of a world weakened by greed and fear, lies and deceit, an attitude of survival of the fittest, and a corrupt few determined to win regardless of the cost to everyone else. Their master plan is exposed and is unraveling.

Love trumps all, so continue with your willingness or preference to open your heart to your family, friends, and strangers and pave the way into our new paradigm. Be the change agent for peace. Be the one in your family, community, and in your workplace to take the stand and demonstrate how the guidelines and tools in this book work. Ask others to take a chance and play, and see for themselves what results they can experience. Share some of your results as an example and be the leader for change.

My hat is off to all of you who know there has to be a better way, and are willing to do whatever it takes to experience life with an open heart, and eventually help others to do the same.

≈ 19 ≈

Imagine

I T'S TIME FOR ALL OF US to start imagining how we want our lives, our family's lives, and our communities to look, feel, and function. In a perfect world, what do we want? How can we serve, and who needs our help? Imagine your heart opening to the world and feeling safe, empowered, and supported.

John Lennon's song "Imagine" is now possible; we are in the times that he envisioned back in the '60s and '70s. We are living out his vision as we choose to change our minds, accept what is, forgive the past, and imagine all the good things we want to be, experience, and enjoy.

How It Can Work

A client this week walked into my office for his first one-on-one business coaching session. Let's call him Robert. His heart was wide open and yet he felt stuck, restless, and full of anxiety trying to conform to the old ways of our world. Robert was stifling his creativity and big heart with the need to fit in, and not show up his friends and colleagues.

His whole life, he knew he was different, yet he fought the difference with all his might.

The first thing I did was to acknowledge his heart, and then explain how authentic leadership works. Robert started to relax and let go of some of the bottled-up emotions he had been carrying around for so many years. The tears rolled down his cheeks as he remembered his soul's promise to bring peace to his world.

I encouraged him to start leading the pack with his heart and to honor the fact that he was already measuring success by how in touch with his heart he was. Yet he had such judgments on this measure.

We talked about how money and things don't buy love and happiness; about how all those people he was trying to conform with may have an abundance of money and things, but what they really want is love—they want to feel their hearts.

Robert was able to gradually change his thoughts and beliefs about conforming and leadership and to understand that he already has the success the whole world is looking and searching for! He now sees that leadership is about going first through modeling and mentoring; that being willing to take that chance and step out from the crowd empowers others to do the same. Conformity enables them to stay put.

Robert emailed the following feedback from our session. I received his permission to share it with you.

> Doug,
>
> That session was powerful and I feel impelled to go further down this road.
>
> The process of first recognizing then acknowledging and eventually resolving internal blocks kinda reminds me of sorting out a pile of tangled rope.

At first you are grabbing it at random places trying to figure out where the hitch points are and where one rope starts and another ends.

Next you start to get a sense of scope and feel your way through the knots releasing the obvious and easily accessible . . . And eventually you get to the ones you wonder if you will ever release . . . These are the ones that have worked against themselves to the point that they are incredibly tight and bound and almost impossible to see where they start or end.

At this point it is easy to decide that these ones are too tightly bound or complex to deal with and throw the whole mess out . . . But the fun and challenge is to work your way through these. Tugging here . . .Twisting there. . . and finally it just becomes obvious how the line lays and how the last of it must be worked. With diligence and focused effort you finally work it free. I suspect in my case I am currently still poking and prodding the rope.

I actually gain great satisfaction in untangling ropes and my wife generally hands me a pile of tangled necklaces knowing that I will get them sorted and enjoy doing so.

Robert

And then Robert sent the following a few minutes later:

Re-reading what I just sent . . . Something came to me. I missed the most important part in the first statement . . . I not only felt impelled to go further—I am at the point where I am permitting myself to go forward. Way too often, I have run up against my own doubts, fears, or preconceived notions and held myself back from what I intuitively knew was the right direction for me.

Our discussion is helping me to see this and I now know that this is one of the first knots I must release.

Robert

Wow, I can't wait for session two. We will now be able to start to play in his heart and help create his business and service from this new perspective. He has all the success of the world in his heart, and he has his heart open! I said to him, "The world needs you, the business world needs you."

People are literally dying out there because of the state of our world, and without courageous leaders like my client, there is no hope.

Love Is All There Is

When I was hiking up the watershed with my friend Otis later that day, some lyrics from a Bon Jovi song, "What do you got, if you ain't got love," were playing in my mind for most of our hike. It's so sad to think that success would be measured any other way than love, wholeheartedness, joy, and peace. What have I got if I don't have my heart open? Nothing.

Over the past few years, every time I heal a grievance, a painful experience, or a downright tantrum through my training, I feel humbled. The first thing that pops into my mind is, "Only the healing matters, only love matters," not a damn thing else. Not my home, car, toys, beliefs, thoughts, or differences with others. None of that matters, only the healing and love do.

Then I get back rolling in my life and forget how humbled I was, and I end up in another grievance, another misunderstanding, or feeling past pain, or simply finding myself in judgment of someone else and their actions. Oops. It's time to surrender and do my healing work again. What have I got if I ain't got love?

Imagine a world where each one of us pulled back just one judgment a day from our intimate relationships, from our core family, from one friend, then from a community or organization. What would our world look like?

What would happen if we all started taking back our judgments and forgiving ourselves for putting them out there in the first place? I feel peace when I imagine a whole new paradigm, one of understanding, cooperation, support, creativity, and friendship. Friendship with those we do not even know, as we recognize they are doing the same thing, pulling their judgments and projections back and using forgiveness.

Imagine what your life would be like without so many grievances. Without so many people who are wrong or bad. As a player, it's your responsibility to step out of the crowd and model authentic leadership, to mentor others who are willing to experience this new paradigm. Believe me, others will notice and want some! They will ask you for guidance and be so appreciative that you took the chance and had the courage and the willingness to forgive when the pain was so deep.

Imagine all of us helping each other; being account-able for our own healing and understanding. No one else can take the step to pull back our judgments and projec-tions. If we don't, we stay stuck, and worse, we enable those we love to stay stuck too!

Imagine a world where there is no hope. What would that be like? Get right into the feeling of no hope, and no use. We are all doomed. Now imagine from your heart what your world could be like with forgiveness as your path.

Start to feel your soul and the passion inside that so wants to open in you. Feel the love from within and start to see a world that truly makes your heart sing. As you commit to forgiveness and creating your world in this new paradigm, keep seeing yourself and everyone else finding a more peaceful way to live.

Imagine you had no blocks, no money issues, no stress, and no worries. What would your life look like? Ask yourself this question, "If money was no object, what would I be doing?" Let the answer come in from your intuition. It may take a few days or hours, or be instan-taneous. Just let the answer come in. Looking for the answer in your mind will be futile, and you will try to answer the question with the same mind that created the money attachment. Go with the first thought that came in—this is your intuition!

You can also use the question and replace money with anything that you feel bound to or that dictates how you live. If politics was no object, what would I be doing? If my partnership or marriage was no object, then what? If my job was no object, what would I be doing? Imagine putting anything in this question that you feel blocked by or attached to. What would your life look like?

Remember the story earlier about the elephant? All he had to do was walk away. His rope was attached to a small stake in the ground.

Imagine pulling back one judgment a day from a world leader in politics, banking, or business. What would the world be like if we all did this? Our world leaders would start to feel our love, we would be forgiving and healing ourselves, and they would naturally start to wake up and see a better way. We need to be leaders who model forgiveness, kindness, and understanding, mentors who support others who have lost their way.

Imagine now, if you will, your life, your family's life, your community, and your country. How would you like to shape these? What is your heart's vision for them? Feel into this and stay pointed in that direction, use the guidelines, tools, and tracking systems set out in this book.

Forgive yourself when you forget, and forgive everyone, from those who are fully asleep to those who forget once in a while, like us.

Let's all play this new game. If we do not lead with our hearts, who will?

My love is with you as you pioneer your way in our new paradigm. Please remember, even I will forget The Miracle of Change game guidelines and tools once in a while, so please be my friend and gently remind me when this happens. Please extend yourself to me with understanding and forgiveness when I fall back asleep, for I am doing the best I can with what I have.

Thank you, I love you.

About the Author

Doug Anderson, founder of 21st Century Dynamics®, is a Psychology of Vision (POV) trainer and a life coach specializing in business coaching and leadership training. He is a member of the POV International and Canadian trainers teams, a member of the International Coaching Federation, and a student of A Course In Miracles.

Doug is a visionary, a leader, and a pioneer with a clear and realistic understanding of our current times. His powerful communication style and skills, empathy and understanding, combined with life experience and training in humanistic psychology, uniquely qualify him to offer this timely opportunity for positive change to the people he serves.

Doug loves blending humor with real life experience and works from the premise that life balance plays a major role in one's overall success. Accountability, directness, enthusiasm, and intuition are some of his personal strengths.

He was born in Calgary Alberta, Canada in 1959, raised in Vancouver British Columbia (since 1960) and currently lives on the Sunshine Coast, British Columbia enjoying nature and the outdoors in his free time.

Doug's background includes a very successful twenty-two-year residential real estate career. During that time, he served on and chaired corporate and charity boards. He has received numerous industry awards, including life membership in the Greater Vancouver Real Estate Board's MLS Medallion Club and the Chris O'Brian Award of Excellence.

Visit him online at: *www.douganderson.ca; www.21stcenturydynamics.com* or *www.povcanada.com*